W9-BZM-121

# Managing Academic Change

*Interactive Forces and Leadership*
*in Higher Education*

*S. V. Martorana*
*Eileen Kuhns*

With a Foreword by
Fred F. Harcleroad

# MANAGING
# ACADEMIC
# CHANGE

Jossey-Bass Publishers
San Francisco · Washington · London · 1975

MANAGING ACADEMIC CHANGE
*Interactive Forces and Leadership in Higher Education*
by S. V. Martorana and Eileen Kuhns

Copyright © 1975 by: Jossey-Bass, Inc., Publishers
615 Montgomery Street
San Francisco, California 94111
&
Jossey-Bass Limited
3 Henrietta Street
London WC2E 8LU

Library of Congress Catalogue Card Number LC 74-27909

International Standard Book Number ISBN 0-87589-253-1

Manufactured in the United States of America


JACKET DESIGN BY WILLI BAUM



FIRST EDITION

*Code 7505*

The Jossey-Bass Series
in Higher Education

# Foreword

In *Issues of the Seventies,* published at the beginning of this critical decade, I noted that the United States has one of the oldest existing governments. "In order to last this long, our society has been extremely flexible and has adapted to the enormous changes which have taken place in the past twenty decades" (Harcleroad, 1970, p. ix). The strength of our citizenry, the possibilities of expansion in our developing West, and our extensive natural resources made such changes possible. Today, however, the revolution of rising expectations finds the nation and the world short of some critical resources, and the shortages have brought about an expanding inflation. Because aspirations are now higher than available necessities, change and innovation in society must develop in a far different context. This stress is particularly true in higher education. In a time of limited expansion and growth, how can we improve education and expand creative opportunities for learning?

In *Managing Academic Change,* S. V. Martorana and Eileen Kuhns present a provocative and systematic answer by combining theory and practice in a Darwinian analysis of changes in many colleges and universities. Their analysis may very well lead in future years to a demonstrable theory of evolution in such institutions. As they point out, change in existing institutions is necessary not only to meet the needs of society but to ensure institutional survival as well.

In the history of higher education, thousands of institutions have died aborning, but thousands more have closed their doors after decades or even centuries of service because they did not change. In contrast, those that survive are those that have adapted. For example, one hundred and fifty years ago George Ticknor, a recently appointed member of the small faculty of Harvard College, was able to institute some small but significant changes there—changes which made it possible for Harvard to grow between 1828 and 1870. Ticknor's small changes included the introduction of an elective system for upper-division students, the development of collegiate departments, and the division of students into groups which would be "encouraged to proceed as rapidly as may be found consistent with thorough knowledge of the subjects of their studies." These reforms were the result of widespread student protest over the existing restrictive classical curriculum. They were modest in scope, but they were sufficient to make Harvard attractive enough to students so that it grew while other colleges stagnated.

The observation of Martorana and Kuhns that the focus of the world of academe, as at Harvard, has to change with societal changes leads them to a "marketplace" theory of higher education that emphasizes the increasing power of the consumers of education rather than the producers. Among the resulting changes that they foresee in coming years is a move toward the separation of academic functions and disciplines rather than their continued integration in comprehensive all-things-to-all-people institutions which have become characteristic of our educational system in recent decades. They sense a trend back to direct experience through work-study, cooperative education, internships, off-campus study, and other forms of action learning, in which the total community serves as an educational facility. Likewise, they see increased interest in affective education. They are concerned, however, that much current innovation "is projected on minimal bases of research and also provides minimally for management and evaluation of results"; they argue convincingly that the evaluation of innovation must become systematic, analytic, and habitual.

Survival is a strong instinct, even for institutions—as the current crisis in financial and moral support for postsecondary education has revealed. The authors make a significant contribution to the likelihood of institutional survival by basing their theory of academic change on sound philosophical underpinnings and by applying it to twenty various institutions in sufficient detail to help readers measure the change possibilities in individual institutions. Further, they focus on the developmental stages through which innovations progress. And, finally, they emphasize the many forces which have critical impact on institutions, such as governmental legislation, external accreditation, leadership personnel, and institutional goals. Some of these forces are almost impossible to control. Through their interactive forces theory, they provide a systematic tool for educators to use in assessing these forces and in trying to adapt to them to assure that their institutions remain viable.

All in all, with their ideas and examples in this unusual book, Martorana and Kuhns should contribute significantly to the survival of the fittest of our academic institutions.

FRED F. HARCLEROAD
*Professor of Higher Education*
*University of Arizona*

# Preface

Persons who wish today to lead the academic community toward greater effectiveness in meeting the social goals set for it must cope with change that is ubiquitous, penetrating, and inescapable. These leaders are increasingly realizing that ways to manage change are sorely needed. The need is both for better mechanisms to handle change in day-to-day operations and for sound management principles and social science theory; only with this basis can change for the sake of change and the consequent waste of scarce resources be avoided. In addition, leaders in colleges and universities need to see the change process as a gestalt—a process having an integrity and definable character rather than a scattered, segmented phenomenon. This book responds to these needs.

The idea for *Managing Academic Change* originated in a conversation with the administrative staff of an Education Professions Development Act (EPDA) summer institute at Fort Hays

State College in Kansas, where we were invited to serve as consultants. One of the main concerns of the faculty members and administrators attending the institute was the problem of change in colleges and universities—how it takes shape and direction, and how changes that have real effect can be differentiated from merely random and ineffective groping. Learning of our views about the need for a better understanding of the change phenomenon, John D. Garwood and Calvin E. Harbin advised us to collaborate on a volume devoted to the topic. From this suggestion came our approach to a theory of effective change in colleges and universities.

During the next two years, we spared no colleagues in higher education our questions about their acquaintance with innovative ventures. We asked people who were identified with provocative innovations to draft statements about their change and its origins; and, on learning about our project, other educators asked to participate by describing innovations at their institutions. Ultimately, authors at some two dozen institutions submitted reports on innovations covering the full range of academic concerns from students and curriculum to facilities and finance. These descriptions of academic change appear in Chapters Two through Five; and, as a consequence of these contributions, this book is a distillation of many minds much more than a creation only of our own.

As the reports began to arrive, two unplanned results emerged. First, the innovations described seemed to fall into four general change patterns: the creation of new campus-based institutions, the development of noncampus alternatives, the organization of satellites to existing institutions, and the reform of existing programs. Second, a theory of change in higher education began to evolve from the experiences reported in these case studies, a theory of interactive forces, which we present in detail in Chapter Eight.

Two years later we returned to Fort Hays for an informal field test of this interactive forces theory as a tool for understanding change. Representatives from eleven colleges (different from those in the case studies) applied our ideas to innovations in their own institutions: innovations ranging from nonpunitive grading and faculty evaluation of administrators to mini-courses in mathematics and the use of behavioral objectives. This test encouraged us to believe that an interactive forces theory can be used by faculty members and administrators to assess and better understand prospects for change on their own campuses.

Since then we have had opportunities to apply our theory firsthand to changes in other institutions. As a result, this book has become more than the originally intended handbook of reports on significant innovations and the means by which they were implemented; it now includes a related general theory of the forces that interact and impinge on any academic innovation.

We intend this book to be helpful to at least two groups of people active in higher education. First are decision makers themselves—administrators, faculty members, trustees, and officials in state systems and statewide planning and coordinating boards—who must stimulate change to fulfill constructive goals, guide the processes of change, and evaluate the results of change. Second are the scholars and analysts of institutional change—sociologists, economists, political scientists, and professors of higher education—who require both base examples and theory for their studies of colleges and universities.

With these readers in mind, we have organized the volume into two major parts. We open with a chapter that illustrates the current intensity of change in higher education and indicates why change will be a necessary characteristic of colleges and universities in the foreseeable future. Chapters Two through Five contain examples of the four different approaches to academic change mentioned earlier: new campus-based institutions, new institutions employing open education as an alternative to the campus, institutions developing adjuncts or satellites as relatively autonomous structures, and institutions implementing major reforms within their existing structures. In these chapters the authors of the cases describe their innovations; we introduce the examples by relating them to the wider scene of higher education and by summarizing their salient features.

In the second part of the book, Chapter Six interprets these cases in light of ongoing trends in American higher education; Chapter Seven introduces guidelines for campus change leaders based on these cases and discusses the use of strategies and tactics

to effect change; Chapter Eight illustrates how our theory of interactive forces can be used to effect similar changes and considers the
utility of theory as a tool for further academic innovations.

In closing this prefatory statement, we wish to thank the
many persons who have helped us in this work. Besides the case
writers, who have been gracious in their willingness to revise their
statements and approve our editorial suggestions for the purposes of
this book, we wish to thank specifically Fred F. Harcleroad, for his
vote of confidence in agreeing to write the Foreword even before
seeing the completed manuscript, and G. Lester Anderson, JB Hefferlin, and G. Kerry Smith for reading the manuscript and suggesting
many helpful improvements. Carrie Mae Martorana deserves credit
for the clarifications she helped us make in the matrix scoring procedure and the mathematical rationale for it, as does E. Douglas
Kuhns for his helpful suggestions on institutional goals as a factor
in assessing change. The administrators of the EPDA workshops at
Fort Hays State College merit our thanks for sensitizing us to the
need for a book on the management of change and for permitting
the test of our theory at the second workshop; in this regard our
indebtedness to the workshop participants needs also to be emphasized. Finally, we are indebted in many ways to our employers,
Pennsylvania State University and the American Association of
Community and Junior Colleges, for their understanding, encouragement, and support.

We dedicate this book and the effort it represents to our
families in recognition of their fundamental faith in higher education and in people.

*University Park, Pennsylvania*                    S. V. Martorana
*Washington, D.C.*                                 Eileen Kuhns
*January 1975*

# Contents

# Managing Academic Change

*Interactive Forces and Leadership
in Higher Education*

# I

# Innovation: Necessity or Fad?

$V$irtually every American college is currently trying out new ideas to improve its programs and operations (see Heiss, 1973; Cornell University, 1974). Admissions requirements and degree requirements, freshman orientation and the Ph.D. dissertation, the liberal arts college and the professional school, the academic calendar, the use of campus facilities—all are being reexamined. Samuel B. Gould, recently the chairman of the Commission on Non-Traditional Study, describes the reactions of educators and educational institutions to this pressure for innovation: "Some are defensive, some noncommittal, some aggressive to the point of fierceness. The only characteristic they have in common is the need to react in some

1

*way;* nobody dares to ignore what is happening whether or not he agrees with it" (Gould, 1972, p. 178).

Even the fundamental concept of higher education itself is affected. The *Higher Education Amendments of 1972,* for example, in its specific provisions refers recurrently not to "higher" education but to "postsecondary" education. Principles of egalitarianism are increasingly outweighing those of selectivity and elitism; and "the idea of the university" is today very different from that as recently as the turn of the century (Ashby, 1974).

## Factors Creating Demands for Change

For many reasons, the decades of the 1970s and the 1980s seem destined to be marked as particularly innovative in the history of higher education. Critical and fundamental shifts are occurring in American society and in the economy, and colleges and universities will have to cope with their ramifications: changes in public attitude, financial support, student enrollment, and operating procedures. The principal factors which are combining to create the demand for change in higher education need not be reviewed at length here. Other volumes are devoted to their description, analysis, and interpretation (for example, see Carnegie Commission, 1972b; Heilbroner, 1974; Snow, 1969). But a few selected factors merit brief discussion.

*Rising expectations.* The UNESCO report *Learning to Be,* called by one authority the "most important document on education in this decade and possibly in this quarter century" (Houle, n.d., p. 56), indicates an emerging worldwide value shift with respect to education. Specifically, it views the student as a lifelong learning consumer and the faculty member as a learning facilitator:

> Every individual must be in a position to keep learning throughout his life. The idea of lifelong education is the keystone of the learning society.
>
> The dimensions of living experience must be restored to education by redistributing teaching in space and time.
>
> Education should be dispensed and acquired through a multiplicity of means. The important thing is not the path

an individual has followed, but what he has learned or acquired.

Teaching, contrary to traditional ideas and practice, should adapt itself to the learner; the learner should not have to bow to preestablished rules for teaching.

Any system according educational services to a passive population and any reform which fails to arouse active personal participation among the mass of learners can achieve at best only marginal success [Faure and others, 1973].

*Public disenchantment.* Strong and general endorsement of the values of education to a democratic society is an American characteristic. Until the late 1960s higher educational institutions in America rode the wave of this tide. Then, for a variety of reasons, public attitudes and support for higher education turned from positive advocacy to negative criticism. "Higher education stands accused of poor planning, of being insensitive to the needs of society, of ignoring recent technological developments that could make teaching more effective, of being unable to provide valid information on its operations, of ineffectual use of resources" (Bogard, 1972, p. 9). Only drastic changes, according to many critics, will remove these weaknesses.

*Pressure for accountability.* Accountability has now become an educational watchword. "Cost-benefit analysis" carries with it the obvious implication: maximize the benefits for a given cost. In this context, educators are "accountable" for carrying out their tasks in an efficient and effective manner; and faculty accountability (in institutions which are not research-oriented) is directly and primarily tied to one output measure: the success of students in achieving stated objectives for a course, a program, or a degree. Accountability is most easily discharged when these objectives are performance-based. As a result, the new accountability is demanding increased attention to educational performance, and a systems approach to learning is becoming a virtual prerequisite to accountability.

*Competition for students and dollars.* No stimulus to change can be greater than the sense of a need to survive. And survival is a real question among many colleges and universities, which are facing declining enrollments and reduced funds. "The money crisis in higher education is indeed real," Earl Cheit reported to the Car-

negie Commission on Higher Education in 1972 (p. 144). "Almost
no school is immune from its effects." He predicted that the result
would be large-scale and serious examination by colleges of their
priorities in programs, services, and operations. Intervening years
have borne out his prediction.

   *A different student body.* Changing social conditions as well
as growing competition for students among institutions are producing a number of important trends in the composition of student
bodies. The student population is shifting toward older persons, a
growing proportion of women, and larger numbers of educationally
and economically disadvantaged persons. More than twelve million
Americans are now enrolled in some form of adult and continuing
education. At the same time, the interest of college-age students is
shifting toward occupational education—often in community colleges and technical schools rather than the more conventional
colleges, because the community colleges and technical schools are
considered more flexible and provide more direct preparation for
job entry. Moreover, "open-access" and "open-enrollment" programs, along with financial aid and developmental studies to overcome a poor economic and educational background, are bringing
many more "new students" into postsecondary education. On the
basis of her recent study of these students, Patricia Cross remarks,
"It is time to look for a better approach. The challenge ahead is
not to convert the new learners to traditional learners, but to convert traditional education to a new education that will serve all of
us better" (Cross, 1973, p. 9).

   *Student insistence on flexibility.* Closely related to changes
in the student body are new demands for flexibility in modes of
instruction and in relating educational programs with life experiences. The advantages of proprietary schools in this regard are
becoming noticeable; their practices of short-term, job-related,
direct-experience training—once considered of questionable value in
producing defensible educational results—are being reevaluated.
Private foundations and government agencies are lending prestige
and financial support to nontraditional approaches of integrating
work and study.

   *Concern for affective-learning values.* Psychologists have long
recognized the importance of a feeling of self-worth and of an

encouraging, supportive environment in creating and sustaining motivation for learning. Since the mid-1960s a number of colleges have made these concerns an integral part of their educational approach. The resulting courses are called humanistic education, human development, human potential, and so on. The importance of the total learning environment—the individual and his knowledge, attitudes, values, perception of himself and others—is a common thread uniting affective education. The work of Bloom and others (1964) alerted the academic community to various types of learning: cognitive, psychomotor, and affective. Today, changes in American values are increasing the importance of the quality of life, which usually is a central concern of affective education. For example, respondents to surveys have shifted their perceptions of the major reasons for American greatness. Reasons such as industrial know-how and scientific progress, ownership of private property, hard-working people, and rich natural resources are now giving way to such reasons as equal opportunity for all races, better international relations, government regulation of business abuses, and free education for all qualified (Harris, 1973). All these items reflect a concern for the affective domain and have great implications for continuing change in higher education.

*Developments in technology.* Television, video and audio cassettes, radio, computers, and combinations of these devices are increasingly being used—both in support of conventional instruction and for direct teaching through auto-tutorial approaches. The result is an intense pressure on colleges and universities to adopt new instructional methodologies which capitalize more fully on these technologies and which deemphasize traditional classroom lectures and demonstrations. As stated by the Carnegie Commission (1972a, p. 86), "We are confident that the expanding instructional technology will improve learning, make learning and teaching more challenging to students and teachers alike, and yield cost savings as it becomes more widely used and reduces the need for live instruction. It may, indeed, provide the best means available to us for solving the difficult problem of continuing to educate growing numbers of students of all ages within a budget the American people can afford."

*Federal programs.* Since the early 1960s, the impact of

federal funding programs on American higher education has been impressive; and the influential force of federal programs will undoubtedly continue to be felt (Leslie, Martorana, and Fife, 1975). The federal government is emphasizing financial aid programs to serve the needs of minority and disadvantaged students. It has also stressed specific manpower programs such as those associated with allied health and community services. More important, it is providing funds for experimentation, and in the process it is exercising direct influence over the course of innovation for the future.

*Shift to buyer's market.* All of these forces lead to one basic conclusion about educational change: "Changes inside the educational system come primarily from the outside. The society and the goals it has set for itself exert the pressures, assert the demands, and supply the funds for what the society wants done" (Taylor, 1971, p. 56). And the reason why these outside pressures seem so influential today—compared, for example, to a decade ago—is that in the past ten years, except for a few highly selective institutions and programs, American higher education has shifted from the enviable position of being in a seller's market (having more applicants than places for them) to that of a buyer's market (having more places than students to fill them) (Hefferlin, 1969, pp. 146–147). For faculty members, the same condition prevails as a result of the overproduction of Ph.D.s and the slackening off of enrollment growth: their seller's market of the 1960s has become a buyer's market of the 1970s.

These circumstances undoubtedly affect the climate for academic change, presenting the opportunity for more experimentation. At the same time, these factors also increase the possibility of change for the sake of change, as faculty members, administrators, and boards of trustees search, sometimes desperately, for any kind of change that might help their institution survive. The tide of innovation sweeping over colleges and universities is characterized more by action than by evaluation of action in light of goals. The pressure and the temptation to try new practices is almost universal; yet persons responsible for leadership, direction, and improvement of the effectiveness of higher education frequently lack the analytic evidence and well-developed theoretical concepts which help assure that institutional changes accomplish institutional intentions.

In the past, planned change has seldom been the adaptive mechanism chosen by colleges and universities. A laissez-faire approach has sufficed instead. But in the buyer's market of the 1970s and 1980s, systematic planning and leadership in change will be instrumental to the health if not the survival of many institutions.

## Leaders and Followers of Change

Like most movements in education, the drive for innovation has its special advocates. These are the carriers of the idea of change —the energizers of its process and the instrumentalities for its expansion. Such colleges and universities as Antioch, Bennington, City Colleges of Chicago, the University of Chicago, and Stephens College have been noted for their contribution to new ideas. Some of them seek quite deliberately to separate themselves from more conventional institutions. In the words of Jencks and Riesman (1969, pp. 501–502), they are "eagerly idiosyncratic" and "in revolt against the hegemony of the graduate schools and the triumph of the academic revolution." Antioch College, for example, reached fame as a center for innovation and experimentation in higher education and has been the focus for the Union for Experimenting Colleges and Universities in such ventures as the "University Without Walls" program. Similarly, the League for Innovation in the Community College is a national consortium of junior college districts which aims through cooperative work "to encourage and evaluate innovation and experimentation designed to improve varied aspects of college operations" (*Innovation,* 1972) ; and the recently formed task force of Cooperative Assessment of Experiential Learning institutions (including Empire State College, Thomas A. Edison College, and Minnesota Metropolitan State College among its nine members) aims to develop, test, and utilize new methods of education and evaluation. Individuals such as Samuel B. Gould and Samuel Baskin serve as influential individual carriers and advocates of innovation between and among a variety of institutions.

But by and large, most changes in colleges and universities are not innovations from within but rather borrowings and imitations from other institutions, such as those mentioned above. As indicated by Hertzler years ago, changes in social institutions in general are the result of the diffusion of ideas throughout a communication network (Hertzler, 1947). This fact accounts for the possibility of uncritical adoption of passing fads within education. "The real enemy of successful innovation in any field," Stephen K. Bailey, vice-president of the American Council on Education, has said, "is untempered enthusiasm leading to transcience and disillusionments of faddism" (Bailey, 1972, p. 172)'; and he warns institutions of the dangers of projected technological miracles, fiscal naiveté, and academic shoddiness. Some observers (for example, Mayhew and Ford, 1971) conclude, in fact, that few real changes are occurring within higher education and that most current changes are unrealistic and likely to be short-lived. Moreover, if less successful institutions merely mimic the more successful, and if programmatic shifts merely follow the prospect of new funding sources, the result will continue to be what Riesman (1958) has termed "academic isomorphism," the increased homogenization of higher education, which critics such as Hodgkinson (1971), Newman (1971), and Pace (1974) have decried.

Change for the sake of change—that is, without regard to whether the proposed change will accomplish institutional goals more effectively than current practice—already tends to be the norm. It is unlikely to benefit either institutional survival or student learning, and it is especially dangerous when the process of change takes the form of reaction to one crisis after another. Harried administrators often feel that the time they spend in "putting out fires" leaves little energy for more systematic planning of change; and the concomitant all too often is the introduction of random changes —of anything which shows promise of increasing enrollments or bringing in more resources or solving any other immediate difficulty. Such a "band aid" approach is liable to set in motion inappropriate changes completely unrelated to the goals of the institution and which in the long run may prove to be more liability than asset.

In short, the state of the art of stimulating and directing effective innovation in colleges and universities is not yet adequate for the tumultuous times ahead in higher education. Change is being pursued mainly as a reactive response to immediate problems; most of the energy for change is concentrating on the initiation of the process rather than on its assessment and evaluation; there is a dearth of information about effective change processes; and there is little effort to apply the information that does exist from such basic social sciences as sociology and psychology.

It is the purpose of this volume to help rectify this condition in order to permit more effective and orderly change in higher education in the future. To this end, we explore and discuss the process of planned change in higher education, illustrate various approaches now underway in higher education to planned change, and offer a theoretical approach to the analysis of forces impinging on proposals for change. Academic decision makers need to be able to plan and implement changes consonant with the goals of their institution. They also need to be masters of the art of institutional self-renewal. "As we seek to bring the education we offer into better tune with the times," Paul C. Reinert, president of St. Louis University, has said, "we must remember that the times will continue to change. One basic objective should be to find ways of institutionalizing change on our campuses, of creating processes for continuing self-examination, measurement, and innovation" (1972, p. 22). The following chapters offer cases and a conceptual framework as a working tool to this end.

# II

‗‗‗‗‗‗‗‗‗‗‗‗‗‗‗‗‗

# Creating New
# Campus Institutions

According to Machiavelli, new structures should be created only when existing structures lack the capacity to produce the same results. If such capacity already exists, he contended, no new departure is necessary; instead, the present structures should be made to fulfill their existing potential. This is good advice for innovators in higher education as in any other area of life. Modifying the present system—changing an established institution, adapting an existing program—can often be more effective in achieving results than constructing a totally new system.

Sometimes, however, new beginnings are necessary. In his volume *Exit, Voice, and Loyalty,* Hirschman has explored the conditions under which innovators choose the drastic option of exiting

—of abandoning an operating institution in favor of creating a new one—rather than continuing to try to bring about reform by voicing suggestions for change. He finds that the difference is determined largely by loyalty to the present institution: while loyalty and hope remain, "loyalty holds exit at bay and activates voice" (1970, p. 78); otherwise, the innovator looks elsewhere to put his concepts into practice. The history of higher education repeatedly illustrates the tension between these options. Often educators have succeeded in modifying the policies and practices of existing colleges and universities: convincing them to undertake new tasks, offer new programs, respond to new conditions. But sometimes they have had to risk being accused of disloyalty to their institution by turning instead to the creation of a competing one: a new college or university on a new model.

At certain periods in American history, the time has been ripe for such new institutions. One such period has just passed. During the 1960s hundreds of new colleges were opened to accommodate the bulge of college students born after World War II; and innovative teachers and administrators, if they were dissatisfied with the chances for reform where they worked, could quickly find more favorable surroundings elsewhere. Funds were available and students were plentiful. At other times, however, innovators have been forced to search extensively even for minimal funds and to persuade students to try something new. Prospects for their success have not been bright: financial patrons have been scarce; students have been suspicious; and existing institutions have questioned the legitimacy of the new. Yet creative educators continue to launch new ventures through new institutions, hoping to create an alternative to present institutions and, possibly, if it proves successful, to serve as a model for them eventually to emulate.

Four such new institutions are described in this chapter. These colleges represent four quite different attempts to meet the educational needs of the young-adult years and the middle years, but all of them illustrate a determination to adapt traditional academic forms in order to meet these needs rather than merely reproduce conventional forms. Among the four are a unique new "middle college" for high school students, a professional college for teaching new careers in the human services, a state-supported upper-division college emphasizing interdisciplinary study, and a new community college organized on a cluster model.

Simon's Rock is an experiment of "total immersion" in order to improve school and college articulation for the benefit of student growth. It seeks to reach this goal more directly than other existing attempts at articulation, such as high school and college agreements for bridging the senior year of high school and efforts to allow college freshmen to complete their freshman work early through a modular curriculum; and it has broader aims than merely time shortening, as illustrated by the three-year baccalaureate. Such approaches are almost always ancillary to the conventional programs offered by existing institutions, which hedge their bets by trying the new while not abandoning the old. Not so with Simon's Rock. Here total institutional survival hangs on the success of its innovation. Its goal of serving young people (sixteen to twenty years old) "as adults by adults" poses a radical challenge both to conventional colleges and to traditional high schools—a challenge that is beginning to be accepted by other experimental institutions as well.

The College for Human Services highlights several other trends in American postsecondary education that may also require totally new institutions for their accomplishment. It is designed to produce radical new practices in the education of professionals— traditionally one of the most rigid of all educational realms. It aims at close integration of instruction with professional practice, with its professional personnel serving as "coordinator" teachers. And, perhaps most important in the context of this volume, it is continually adapting its methods so that its goals can be better accomplished.

Governors State University incorporates a variety of new methods into a more conventional upper-division structure. As a locus of innovation for the entire Illinois state system of higher education, it has organized various colleges responsible for specific interdisciplinary emphases, divided its academic calendar into time modules of eight weeks in length, emphasized student contracts based on the student's goals, insisted that the objectives and strategies for learning modules flow from this focus on student goals through self-pacing and relating them to the real world, and based its grading on performance objectives by recording only successful achievement on students' transcripts.

Finally, Oakton Community College has sought to adapt the conventional community college model to new needs. It has been organized into four clusters to provide students with a sense of belonging and of personal concern. It has abandoned academic disciplines and other principles of organization as a basis for these clusters in favor of student assignment on the basis of heterogeneity and faculty assignment on the bases of balance and strength in course offerings, specialized skills, and approaches to teaching. Each of its clusters offers a variety of learning strategies for similar courses; and, to assure that students benefit from this diversity, Oakton describes all course sections within each cluster in an informal directory that identifies the course goals, behavioral objectives, learning strategies, and evaluation and grading procedures for each section. As with the other new institutions, it emphasizes learning rather than teaching.

These four institutions also illustrate several facts about innovation at large and the interactive forces that impinge on innovations. They demonstrate the life cycle through which innovations pass as they mature: a life cycle that can be thought of as having at least five identifiable stages: exploration, formulation, trial, refinement, and, finally, institutionalization (see Chapter Eight).

Obviously, the four institutions reported in this chapter have passed from exploration and formulation through trial and into refinement or institutionalization phases. The College for Human Services can be said to have embarked on the exploration stage of a second innovation rather than proceeding into institutionalization. As it has shifted goals from that of training technicians and granting associate degrees to that of educating certified professionals, it has illustrated a deliberate emphasis on exploration for continuous and sequential innovation rather than on firmly establishing and institutionalizing itself as a completed innovation.

Each of these cases also illustrates the fact that the forces that interact on an innovation differ in importance from one developmental stage to another. The founding of Simon's Rock, for example, involved the stimulus of Elizabeth Hall herself, the availability of a physical site, and the promise of continued financial support; but once the idea moved from exploration to formulation, the new faculty became influential forces themselves, followed when students were first admitted, by students as well. Within two more years, Simon's Rock "settled into a pattern," as President Hall describes it; and more recent events including regional accreditation and a new grant from the Carnegie Corporation suggest that institutionalization of its innovation is at hand.

The key forces during the creation of the College for Human Services include the dedication of its president, the availability of grant funds from the Office of Economic Opportunity and the Department of Labor during its precollege stage, and the contractual support of the cooperating human service agencies in New York City as it commenced operation.

Decision makers at the state level in Illinois, as well as top-level university administrators, were particularly important during the exploration stage of Governors State University. During the formulation stage, these administrators and the self-selected "founding father" faculty provided positive support; but when initial evaluations indicated the wisdom of further changes during the trial and refinement stages, some of these faculty became a negative force for more change. The university's students, not always sharing the goals of its decision makers, played largely a neutral role throughout these several developmental stages.

At Oakton, the development of its cluster concept and its distinctive directory to college opportunities stemmed primarily from its chief administrator and the deans, with most faculty and students supporting the ideas throughout their development, and with a majority of trustees being positive in their endorsement.

Clearly, both Simon's Rock and the College for Human Services illustrate deliberate efforts by their creators to provide radically new alternatives to traditional institutions: alternatives that will require major revision in traditional institutions if they are to incorporate the idea. Governors State and Oakton Community College both show how the need for additional educational opportunities in Illinois permitted creative educators to launch distinctive upper-division and two-year institutions rather than simply replicating existing models of these institutions. They expand our notions of such institutions, while Simon's Rock and the College for Human Services challenge our conception of academic higher education at large.

## HIGH SCHOOL–COLLEGE INTEGRATION: SIMON'S ROCK

ELIZABETH B. HALL, *president emerita, Simon's Rock*

Simon's Rock (in Great Barrington, Massachusetts) is often called an "early" or a "middle" college. In fact, it is neither one. Fundamentally, Simon's Rock is established on the proposition that youth of about ages sixteen to twenty constitute a single peer group which requires an integrated collegiate experience instead of the junior and senior years in a high school and the freshman and sophomore years in a college or university. It would like to be regarded simply as a college in the sense that this term is accepted as adequate preparation for graduate study or professional specialization. It tolerates the adjectives *early* and *middle* merely to differentiate itself, as public authorities require, from traditional four-year senior colleges and, for the sake of public understanding, from two-year junior colleges. But in essence it conceives itself as embodying three convictions which should operate as a force for reform throughout American education: hastening maturity, shortening time for liberal education, and reorganizing educational structure.*

### Rationale

Today's youth possess physical and intellectual powers greater than those of their counterparts in previous generations. Advances in medicine, nutrition, and child care have provided optimum conditions for physical and mental development. Physio-

* These fundamental concepts, which also gave impetus to the rise of community and junior colleges, were identified by Koos (1947) in his research and writings between 1920 and 1950, which culminated in his development of the "6-4-4" plan for public education.

logically, boys and girls become men and women at an earlier age; in addition, largely because the mass media have augmented the supply of information, the factual foundation for their intellectual development has increased. The rate at which young adults achieve emotional maturity (the ability to disdain instant gratification in favor of larger and less selfish and more remote goals) and social maturity (the ability to empathize with others well enough to work together and achieve goals that none could achieve alone), however, remains the same.

In consequence, a dangerous imbalance has developed between the power of execution on the one hand and sound judgment and effective action on the other. To correct this imbalance, we cannot tolerate a prolongation of childhood. We must rather hasten social and emotional maturation—mainly by putting young persons in situations where they must behave in a mature way. For those beyond age sixteen, the essentially paternalistic child-adult relationship of the American high school is inappropriate; instead, the relationships between these young adults and older adults need to be consciously and determinedly on an adult-to-adult basis. As an example of the implementation of this concept, at Simon's Rock there is a majority of one student on the community council, which is concerned with college rules and regulations. The academic council, responsible for academic policies, has a faculty majority of one, while ad hoc committees usually are composed of approximately half students and half faculty members (Whitlock, 1974, p. 19).

This more adult relationship always has been characteristic of what is understood as "college." Thus, it is indeed college in spirit, substance, and form that we at Simon's Rock urge for students beyond tenth grade. We do not, however, advocate the laissez-faire approach to student life that has characterized the American college campus in the last decade. Instead, we insist that the college must assume responsibility for the total welfare of students. It must provide leadership for the students and set standards for the public as well. Specifically, college administrators should accept their roles as leaders, and the teaching faculty should extend their influence beyond the academic to help create a campus environment in which the finer aspirations of the students—such as a better appreciation of their culture, a sharper insight into the major current political and economic problems our society must face and resolve, and a greater understanding of their personal selves—can be realized. Important at any time, this element is essential if collegiate procedures are to be employed as a means to hasten true maturity.

Prior to the establishment of the B.A. program, the amount of credit awarded a student on transfer and the level at which he could transfer were largely an individual matter. For example, one student was accepted by four graduate schools on the basis of Graduate Record Examination scores, while many others have been credited with up to two years of work "above their traditional grade level on transfer from Simon's Rock" (Whitlock, 1974, p. 18).

If students are introduced earlier to a responsibly managed college program, they should be able to assume earlier the constructive roles in adult society that they long to have and that society needs them to assume. Thus, one to two years of in-school time could be eliminated from the sixteen currently required for the baccalaureate, most readily at the level of the senior year of high school and the freshman year of college. It is questionable whether the amount of time allotted for the completion of a liberal education in the United States was ever necessary. Certain forces in our industrial economy militate to keep young people out of the job market by perpetuating childhood as long as possible. And despite the fact that young people do not "come to a boil" all at the same time, with our concept of levels and of doing time in high school in units of academic years, it is difficult for students to opt out for a term or for a year without penalty on return. To make stopping out easier, institutions should operate the year around.

## From Concept to Practice

Simon's Rock is a liberal arts institution, emphasizing both breadth of knowledge and interdisciplinary relationships. Within this setting, the program at Simon's Rock for an individual student depends both on his own goals and on the year of entry. The student entering after completion of his sophomore year in high school may simply finish his secondary education and then transfer to another college; this path is not recommended by the school. He may also elect to complete his Associate in Arts degree in four years; or he may enter the Bachelor of Arts program, which leads to this degree in four years. The latter program includes distribution requirements, first and fourth year interdisciplinary studies, independent studies, an oral and a written examination, and a senior thesis judged by both internal and external examiners. Students may also enter the school after their eleventh or twelfth grade years, but their options are limited. For example, they can complete the A.A. degree in two years, but are not eligible for the B.A. program; to complete it they would have to remain for three years at the college, during which time they would no longer be members of the sixteen-to-twenty-year-old peer group, a concept central to the Simon's Rock plan (Whitlock, 1974).

Simon's Rock became an institutional entity in the late summer of 1964 as a nonprofit corporation under the laws of the Commonwealth of Massachusetts. The owner of a private estate in Great Barrington deeded two hundred acres to the corporation and provided sufficient capital to build a campus sufficient to the needs of two hundred resident students and to nurse the program through its formative years.

Enjoying full financial independence from the outset, Simon's Rock was thus free to put its ideas into practice without constraint from any outside sources of support. Neither the New England Association of Colleges and Schools, our regional accrediting organization, nor the Massachusetts authorities would permit us to use the term *college*. Hence, the name Simon's Rock, after a large boulder on the property, was chosen from many other possibilities because it could stand by itself without a descriptive term. But without description the task of informing the public about our concept and its rationale was made more difficult.

The two years to September 1966 were spent in organization, construction, promotion, program planning, and recruitment of both faculty and students. Because only one dormitory was ready by September, the school opened with only one class—composed of fifty-six girls who had just completed the tenth grade. Each year thereafter, one more class of similar size was added until the fall of 1970, when we not only admitted boys for the first time but also accepted a limited number of students for admission to two advanced classes. At Simon's Rock, Class One, Class Two, Class Three, and Class Four are used instead of freshman, sophomore, junior, and senior to emphasize the difference between a "middle" college and conventional academic institutions. In June 1970 we had our first commencement. By the sixth year of operation, 1971–72, the calendar had settled into a pattern comprising two thirteen-week semesters, fall and spring, with a six-week mid-winter term during which each student undertook some one study full time, either on or off campus.

Thus, in the decade of its founding, Simon's Rock succeeded in putting its basic educational concepts almost fully into practice. In July 1974 the Massachusetts Board of Higher Education authorized the college to offer the Bachelor of Arts degree. Earlier that same year the New England Association of Schools and Colleges granted accreditation. Although the college has not yet fully implemented its plan for year-round operation, work toward this goal continues. With the support of a $350,000 grant made in the fall of 1972 by the Carnegie Corporation of New York, we are developing library resources, investigating new admissions procedures for reaching a younger age group, and structuring new majors with released faculty time and faculty workshops. The Carnegie grant is also providing for a full evaluation which will test the nature of our student body, the qualities that make for successful performance in an early college, and the academic achievements of the program. The first group of students electing a B.A. option will graduate with that degree in 1976.

## Problems

The main problem at Simon's Rock has been our identity. Prior to regional accreditation, students wondered if they were in a "real" college. Parents wondered, too, and asked how long it would be before we were accredited. In the fall of 1967, the New England Association sent a team of six from their Commission on Independent Secondary Schools to evaluate us for the probationary status they reserve for new institutions. In December they reported that we had been awarded status as a "Recognized Candidate for

Accreditation as an Independent Secondary School." The Commonwealth Board of Education had meanwhile granted us authority to confer the Associate in Arts degree, even though at that time we were apparently in violation of a long-standing rule of the board (the origin of which has been obscured by time) forbidding "high school" and "college" students to be housed together. In December 1969 the integrity of our four-year program (the fact that we were not, as commonly misunderstood, "two years of high school and a junior college") was recognized, and we were awarded status as a recognized candidate for accreditation as an integrated four-year academic institution. Students from Simon's Rock have been accepted at some hundred colleges and universities across the country.

There were some on the faculty who, already uneasy by reason of our anomalous situation, wished to rise in the hierarchy of teaching prestige. To prove Simon's Rock a "college" and themselves "college professors," they assumed some of the less admirable attributes of the American college campus of the 1960s. "I'm not a nursemaid. I'm a teacher." "The administration has no right to regulate." These views were shared with students eager, in their own way, to prove themselves "real college students" in the Berkeley manner. Still we held on, and gradually we were reassured by the realization that the disruptive forces had little staying power. They left us, saying we were "too preppy."

### The Future

The future of Simon's Rock will be determined by our success or failure in winning continued official recognition and public acceptance. It seems safe to predict that the essential idea of "less time with more options" will pervade American education. With a sizable grant from the Carnegie Foundation in 1967, four boys' schools—Andover, Exeter, Hill, and Lawrenceville—studied the proposition for a year. The report, titled *The Liberal Education of an Age Group: 16–20*, was favorable. Signs are everywhere that we are not alone in our thinking. Schools struggle with the senior year. Colleges talk of a three-year baccalaureate. Johns Hopkins takes students headed for the medical profession straight out of junior year of high school into the freshman class. All this points to change, and we feel confident that it will be in the direction of Simon's Rock. It is probably, however, not a new "house of education" that is on the drawing boards. Rather, we suspect, it is a drastic and long-overdue renovation of the old structure.

## HUMAN-SERVICES EDUCATION: COLLEGE FOR HUMAN SERVICES

AUDREY C. COHEN, *president, College for Human Services*
LAURA HOUSTON, *vice-president, College for Human Services*
ALIDA MESROP, *special assistant to the president, College for Human Services*

Preparation for the professions as offered today is irrelevant and overextended and does not begin to meet the needs or solve the problems of our society. Witness our decaying schools, hospitals, and urban areas and our burgeoning welfare rolls. The present system of professional training excludes tremendous numbers of potentially effective careerists and encourages mediocrity by its overwhelming orientation toward collecting academic credits and its almost complete lack of emphasis on actual job performance. The College for Human Services, in New York City, believes that a new measure of a professional based on competence is needed. Two examples of such competence are: the ability to participate effectively in a group, helping to establish clear goals and work toward optimum results; and the ability to function as a supervisor, teaching, encouraging, and enabling human service workers to make the best use of their abilities on behalf of the client. Together, the competences add up to a description of the excellent human service professional. Students do not take the major part of their work as courses. Instead they concentrate on competences, around which the curriculum is organized. To blend theory and practice students spend two days each week at the college and three days a week in supervised field work in a human service agency; there they prepare for positions such as social work assistant, guidance assistant, research assistant, counselor, legal services assistant, community health worker. Students close each day at the college in a field focus group. Here they review the work of the day and discuss how to apply it to solving the problems of clients in the agencies in which they are practicing.

## Time Frame

The College for Human Services began operation in 1966 as the Women's Talent Corps, a one-year antipoverty program for low-income adults, funded by the Office of Economic Opportunity. By the middle of 1968, in direct response to student needs and desires, the college began to develop. In 1969, a second year was added to the program; and intensive negotiations, necessitated by the college's application for a charter, were begun with the New York State Board of Regents. In May 1970, after a struggle in which every facet of the institution participated, the charter battle was won; and the new College for Human Services was officially established, with authority to award an Associate of Arts degree to students who successfully complete its two-year course of study. The college has since undertaken the complex process toward another goal: the awarding of a full professional degree to those who complete the curriculum and demonstrate the effective, competent, professional performance that this degree represents. That this proposition is a viable one is evident in the fact that on June 19, 1974, over seventy-five national leaders met at Columbia University to discuss the formation of a new profession—the human services profession. According to the consensus expressed by that assembly, this new profession is based on three major, interconnecting processes: intensive, telescoped professional preparation which blends theory and practice while focusing on basic competences in the helping fields; assessment which continues throughout the professional career; and increased lay participation in the problem-solving and evaluation processes.

## Principles and Problems

The College for Human Services has, since its inception, operated according to the following principles:

1. We have tried to open new kinds of positions which did not exist prior to our efforts. These jobs have resulted directly from recognized community needs. Students have been trained for and employed as teacher assistants, social work assistants, mental health workers, guidance assistants, and (under a special program with Columbia Law School) legal assistants.

2. We have continually asked ourselves, "What are our institutional goals, and how can the environment be controlled in order to create necessary changes?" Several strategies are involved here. Every participating community-service agency is committed to the college contractually. The contract with the agency guarantees each student a field placement, a preprofessional position at the end of the first year, and a professional position upon successful completion of the second year. Faculty, who are called "coordinator teachers," provide close liaison between the college and the field agency.

3. We believe that any professional who deals directly with people must care—must be humane—and that there must be a synthesis of theoretical knowledge, special skills, and such specific behavioral qualities as tenderness, compassion, and aggression. This need to integrate positive, humanistic attitudes with expert specialized knowledge corresponds to growing indications of a strong movement to restore the individual to prominence. Professionals are needed to help millions of individuals grow and receive justice in an increasingly complex and quickly changing world. To win acceptance, these new kinds of professionals must also be committed to developing a new system of evaluation based on performance competence.

4. We have tried to utilize all past experiences. We have learned, for instance, that many of our graduates, even though they are able to perform on a professional level, do not always receive professional acceptance because they lack a professional credential. Turning this finding to positive action, we are now planning to provide advanced professional specialization.

5. We hope to have a permanent impact—that is, to influence other institutions. There were no models of educational institutions operating in tandem with agencies to think through all the implications of service delivery, to accept the total blending of

theory and practice as a way to arrive at full professionalism, and to award a full professional degree for this method of preparation. Therefore, the college itself assumed the responsibility of building that alternative educational model.

6. We believe in the institution's uniqueness and are committed to clear, long-range goals. The institution remains committed to the whole new concept, not individual elements of this concept which some other colleges have adopted. To the question "Why is the college moving on when what you have done already is so good?" we answer, "The mission is not finished. Total success has not been attained." That success, our long-range goal, is full acceptance by the public as well as the professions of our ideal of a humanistic attitude base from which all practice proceeds.

7. On behalf of students, the college works with unions, the civil service, and other institutions that value degrees as criteria for advancement. At the same time, the college seeks to build an alternative model for establishing legitimacy for a recognized new professionalism; in this attempt it is cooperating with all agencies that are willing to work for change.

When change like that envisioned by the College for Human Services is attempted, there are obviously crisis points, barriers, and problems. Here are some of the problems that we have faced:

1. *Tensions generated by telescoping the time frame of student learning.* The college demands that both students and faculty remain activists for improved delivery of social services to the community. Faculty must remain humane and understanding of students, recognizing that many of the students experience strain and uncertainty because they are seeking professional status through an unorthodox preparation; they need steady and reliable support. The College for Human Services meets this need by giving special attention to faculty and student relationships and to student and agency relationships; the emphasis is constantly to affirm to the student that he will be both employable and able to meet the demands of his job when employed.

2. *Tensions among persons drawn to a philosophy and to an action-oriented program.* These persons are essentially self-selected and are inherently dissenters who have been fighting the status quo for a good part of their lives. Now, as part of an institution which

seeks to implement significant academic changes, they face a new role; instead of rebelling against traditional practices they now must give energy and positive support to making the institution work. This sharp shift in behavior pattern often generates anxiety.

3. *Tensions between a traditional and an innovative approach.* The college prepares new professionals to perform effectively in a human-service agency. The traditionally prepared professional feels challenged and insecure in relating to the new professional. Since the mission of the college to promote service as well as academic institutional change is well known, the tension is exacerbated.

4. *Tensions between college and agency personnel.* Faculty members or specialists at the college often encounter difficulty in relating to outside agency personnel because of their different credentials. These problems are reduced when the human-service agency is directly involved in the curriculum planning.

5. *Tensions of students about rewards.* Students doubt that they will be employed as new professionals at commensurate salaries. The college has found three effective mechanisms to allay these fears: (1) a signed contract between the college and a field-service agency that provides on-the-job training and guarantees placement, (2) involvement of the agency in curriculum design, (3) use of comprehensive field committees, which include agency supervisors, college staff (curriculum specialist, field director, director of research and evaluation, acting dean, and former faculty members) as well as students.

## Productivity

Because the program is small, its success cannot be measured quantitatively. In six program years, from 1967 through 1972 (the first year of operation was as a demonstration project for the Office of Economic Opportunity), approximately 80 percent of all the students came to the college unemployed. Work backgrounds were largely limited to low-income, dead-end jobs. Approximately 50 percent came to the college receiving public assistance.

Of the 747 entering students (1967–1972), 598, or approximately 80 percent, finished the first year. By 1974, just before the new Master's professional program was launched, over six hundred students had completed the first year. Approximately 92 percent of these were immediately placed in human-service positions in community-service agencies, consumer-affairs agencies, day-care centers, schools, health clinics, hospitals, legal-service agencies, social work agencies, research centers, and housing and development. As of December 1972, the college has had the cooperation of over two hundred agencies in training people for the human services. By 1974 over three hundred students had returned on released time from their agencies to complete the second year and to receive A.A. degrees. Approximately one hundred students have enrolled in other institutions of higher education in order to continue their studies.

Certain important results of the program, although they are difficult to quantify, are nevertheless easily observable. For example, the students report improvements in their personal lives—a better ability to cope with the problems of urban living, and even new attitudes of seriousness and responsibility in their children, as if motivation were catching. The statistics showing that these students have stayed on the job and moved into positions of increasing responsibility *imply* a good deal more.

The college also attempts to improve the setting in which students work. A close relationship between college staff and agency supervisors is encouraged. Since 1972, the college has conducted a regular series of workshops for agency supervisors which focus on problems and techniques of supervision. The comprehensive field committees noted above serve also to improve both the college and the agencies. By constructing a thoroughly integrated work-study program, the college helps the field agency become a partner in the education of human service professionals, much as hospitals are teaching institutions for doctors; it helps teachers to become the organizers and coordinators of learning experiences rather than arbiters and dispensers of knowledge.

The college fully expects that specific pieces of its program will be replicated elsewhere. Indeed, this has already happened in some instances. However, the new educational theories embodied at the college involve many new concepts; to test these pieces singly, in a setting which is otherwise traditional, is to test them out of context. For this reason, the college expects to remain an entity and to refine itself continually in order to fulfill its goals.

The college feels that any experimental institution can make a continuing and lasting contribution only if it has somehow built into its operation a theory and method of change. The charter granted to the college by the New York State Board of Regents charges it "to build an educational institution that will remain in the vanguard of educational experimentation." The college regards this duty with utmost seriousness.

## How to Plan

The following planning guidelines, based on the experience of the College for Human Services, can be advanced: (1) The developmental process should involve persons who see the inadequacy of present professional preparation, who sense the need for effective problem solving, and who are committed to change. (2) Community meetings should pinpoint problems which have not been mitigated by the existing human-service agencies. (3) Development of alternative career preparations in specific fields should be limited to two or three areas of concentration. (4) Exploration of funding should consider both governmental and private sources. (5) Since a work-study curriculum is offered, the support of community agencies in opening placements for on-the-job training is critical. (6) Each new institution should have a curriculum specialist on its staff from the very beginning.

## INTERDISCIPLINARY EDUCATION IN CULTURAL STUDIES: GOVERNORS STATE UNIVERSITY

LARRY McCLELLAN, *university professor of urban studies, Governors State University*

DANIEL BERND,* *university professor of English, Governors State University*

* Portions of this section are adapted from an earlier article by Daniel Bernd (1971).

Governors State University, in Park Forest, Illinois, was formally established in July 1969 as an upper-division university mandated to serve the educational needs of the southern half of the Chicago metropolitan complex. Governors State enrolls juniors, seniors, and graduate students who have transferred from junior colleges and other institutions. Its special responsibility to serve the educational needs of low- and middle-income and minority students is exhibited by its interdisciplinary approach, illustrated here by the College of Cultural Studies, which is responsible for the disciplines in language and literature, the social sciences, and the fine arts (including the performing arts).

As defined at Governors State, here are some of the things that an interdisciplinary program is *not:*

1. It is neither antidiscipline nor nondiscipline. The disciplines as disciplines are not necessarily ill conceived or irrelevant. As Dean Saul Cohen of Clark University once said, "Relevance is a problem in education that the disciplines must help to solve—not a quality they either possess or lack."

2. Its faculty members are not "generalists." The expansion of knowledge means specialization. Whatever interdisciplinary studies may be, they cannot provide the rationale for amateurism in education.

3. An interdisciplinary program is not generated by a social value system imposed from outside the disciplines. Dumping a lot of specialists into the same curriculum and labeling it with some honorific title ("democracy," "humaneness") does not produce an interdisciplinary program.

4. Just as the problem of interdisciplinary studies is not that of discovering relevance or of creating new superdisciplinarians, neither is it a solution to the problem of research versus teaching. If the activity of research is essentially the activity of creating knowledge, and if teaching and training have something to do with what happens to that knowledge, then it is difficult to see how the allocation of resources between those two activities is going to be solved by the definition of new programs of interdisciplinary studies. The necessity of making teachers out of researchers and researchers out of teachers will remain with us.

5. An interdisciplinary program is not one in which one or

several disciplines are subsidiary or instrumental to another discipline. That is, interdisciplinary programs do not attempt to meld disciplines, as "core curriculum," "communication," or even "American studies" programs attempt to do.

Instead, the College of Cultural Studies—through a device called the Interdisciplinary Studies Context (ISC)—bases its interdisciplinary program on specific issues or problems that allow several disciplinary perspectives. The problems must be substantive, not merely administrative; and the program must be based on disciplines. Finally, the issues or problems selected must be such that all three disciplinary areas (language and literature, fine and performing arts, and the social sciences) can contribute to them; at the same time, the particular integrity of the individual disciplinarians involved in the study of the problem must be preserved. The first Interdisciplinary Studies Context was called "Popular Culture" and formed a basis for developing others. Some Interdisciplinary Studies Contexts are more broadly gauged than others, and some are more developed than others. At present the college has six in operation. In addition to Popular Culture, there are the Black Studies component of Ethnic Studies, Socio-Cultural Processes, Language and the Human Condition, Invention and Creativity, and Area Studies. Eventually the college will add a seventh ISC, Ideas in Culture.

### Innovative Elements

The academic programs of the college feature several innovative elements.

*Student contracts.* Each student entering the college is assigned a faculty advisor. During the first session, the student and advisor negotiate a contract. Included in this contract are a statement of the student's objectives and needs, an outline of competences to be achieved, and a list of the various learning modules (courses) needed to attain the competences and thus meet the overall contract objectives. A student's individualized program draws on all the resources of the university. Learning modules are frequently developed by faculty members in two or more of the colleges. Each ISC provides a framework for the contracts. Although general patterns of study have emerged, the individualized learning contract, in contrast to the standardized major found in most universities, often contains unique features and means of meeting objectives.

*Performance objectives and competency-based instruction.* Transcripts do not contain grades, records of incompletes, or any indication of learning modules registered for by the student but not finished. The transcript is in narrative form, and the introductory phrase usually states "has demonstrated" or "is able to." Governors State credit equates with a conventional semester credit, but the award of credit is tied to specific performance objectives, which in turn are tied to the specific competencies outlined in the educational programs and the student contracts. It has been possible to arrive at the end competencies based on examinations, written assignments, and discussions. The paradigm is thus: The student has an overall rationale of what he wants to be. In order to reach that goal, the student states educational objectives in terms of GSU mandates and resources. These educational objectives are reachable through the programs—the learning modules (courses). Each program contains a statement of the specific competencies to which it leads. There are several or many pathways to the competencies desired, and the individual contract is a map describing particular choices and paths.

*Faculty conditions.* Faculty throughout the new university recognize the dynamic conditions in the setting. All the faculty are considered university professors; that is, there is no ranking. Outside resource people who teach at the university are all considered community professors. Second, all faculty prepare and negotiate with their college a yearly work-plan agreement, which outlines their responsibilities for the year and serves as one of the primary bases for yearly evaluation. Third, the university has developed a system of seven-year cyclical tenure, which stands somewhere between tenure as it is generally interpreted and multiyear contracts.

*Open environment.* Much of what goes on in the college and in the university reflects a relatively open style. This results in part from the elements described and from the fact that the university has a generally older student body (average age is twenty-eight) and the faculty work in an open office environment. Even the interior architecture of the campus reflects openness. The governance system does this also, having representation from all constituencies within the university and the outside community.

## Strengths, Problems, Solutions

*Strengths.* The structures, concerns, and elements outlined above reflect many of the strengths of the endeavor at GSU. In addition, the faculty would point to a general respect for each other's professional expertise—essential in an interdisciplinary environment—and what they see as an ongoing sense of innovation. Continuing innovation is structured into the ISC framework for curriculum development, into the various levels of the governance systems, and into the ongoing demands for accountability. As an example of structuring for accountability, a detailed Professional Personnel System has been developed which provides basic principles and procedures for professional responsibilities, work agreements, systems of evaluation, salary and cyclical tenure determinations, and appeal processes.

*Problems.* In an institution which rests on the premise that ongoing, formative evaluation offers the only hope of success and survival, it is well to point out the problems and failures. Though the difficulties may arise out of following Emerson's injunction to "make no little plans," and though GSU might not have its problems if it were not trying so many things at once, it has been no easy ride. Three major problems have been encountered.

In the first place, there is no doubt that the university has projected a more ambitious educational program than it can realistically find resources to implement; neither the staff, the buildings, nor the appropriations have expanded as originally planned and hoped for.

Second is the problem of institutional inertia. No matter how new, how dedicated to change, an institution develops a resistance to changing anything its members have already decided. Those who believe themselves to be founding fathers, even in an institution like GSU, become intolerant of those who wish to suggest their own declarations of independence.

A third problem has to do with institutional aspirations versus individual aspirations. Most of the planners and first faculty members came to GSU because they saw many things wrong in American education and thought they had a chance to improve upon it. The individual student, however, is less global in his outlook. The students wish to train themselves for jobs; they want above all to be *certified*, and no matter how much the faculty try to explain that a competency-based curriculum is not the same thing as a credit-accumulation certificate program, they wish the official laying on of hands to take place as soon as possible. Freedom from the tyranny of majors and required courses is not what a good many students want; they want whatever it will take to gain them access to the economic and political power they do not now possess. In other words, the individual student may not be particularly interested in GSU's changes or innovations as compared with other colleges and universities—even though, according to a recent survey, 25 percent of them believe that they would not have had access to higher education if it were not for GSU.

Moreover, no matter how carefully the guidelines, mandates, goals, and programs may be explained to prospective faculty members, once on board they will try (perhaps understandably) to shape the institution to their own security needs. That is, some faculty members interpret the guidelines and mandates to mean that they are supposed to do what in fact they are used to doing. Faculties have an incredible capacity to interpret the latest suggestion for change as a description of what they were already doing. In fairness, to give faculty the responsibility of new curriculum, new governance, and new community relationships attenuates their resources beyond reasonable capacity.

*Solutions.* The diagnoses of the problems suggest some solutions. The administration and the faculty leaders are beginning to consider some rearrangements and rethinking. The fatigue and attenuation that have been the inevitable concomitants of our beginnings—creating a new model for higher education as well as making it operational—are at least partially compensated for by our openness and insistence on evaluation. Three ameliorating conditions have emerged. One is an understanding that much more careful introduction into the GSU system and sets of subsystems must be planned for both students and faculties. In addition to the glories of individually tailored student contracts and almost total curricular freedom, the faculty must begin to face the existential terror of this freedom. It has become clear that more careful, step-by-step, administratively enforced procedures must accompany contracting, program development, and scheduling.

Second, the faculty know that they must rethink the current mandates and goals in order to ensure that they are serving their clientele's needs instead of some abstract principles that may no longer apply. The professional staff meetings are beginning to include more talk about the substantive questions of education, rather than the all-too-frequent academic pattern of petty haggling over the administration's error.

Finally, for most of the staff and students it must be understood that governance is not an end in itself but a means to serve educational purposes. They have worked together long enough to begin to build some trust, so that they can cease protecting their individual turfs and begin to cultivate them. The governance system is one of shared power; it includes representatives of all constituencies within the university and the outside community. There is arising an increased political sophistication, as those groups who had not before exercised political power become more comfortable with it. The administration and the faculties have both come to understand the intimate relationship between governance and academic programs and are becoming more supportive of each other.

## CLUSTER COLLEGE:
## OAKTON COMMUNITY COLLEGE

WILLIAM A. KOEHNLINE, *president, Oakton Community College*

One of the premises on which Oakton Community College was built is the belief that variations in teaching method and learning style should be controlled by the entire college rather than by individual faculty members. Students learn in different ways and at different rates. In a college where there are many sections of each basic course, those sections will differ among themselves. The founding president and deans believed that the benefit to students from systematizing and announcing these differences in advance would warrant the effort and expense of creating a new publication, supplementing the brief description of each course in the college catalog and the mere listing of days, hours, faculty names, and places of meeting in the typical time schedule.

At the beginning of its second year of operation, August 1971, Oakton prepared its first directory of courses and sections. The experience of faculty and students with this tool has been limited, but the subjective evaluation has been so positive that expansion of the idea, rather than abandonment or major revision, seems warranted.

## Historical Context

Oakton Community College began classes in September 1970. Planning and initial implementation of the directory of courses and sections came in January 1971, with the creation of four nondepartmentalized college groups or faculty clusters. Writing and editing of the first looseleaf edition occurred in the spring and summer of 1970. The second edition, published as a tabloid in November 1971, was used throughout the registration period culminating in January 1972. Subsequent editions have appeared each college term.

## Initiating Decisions

As noted, the decision to structure the college in nondepartmental groups and the decision to produce and publish the directory were highly interrelated. Established colleges usually operate within traditional departmental and divisional structures, which are organized to meet instructional needs through standardized groupings of subject matter. This approach is deemphasized at Oakton to facilitate the task of designing programs to meet current needs. Because of this deemphasis of structure and accent on a programmatic view, Oakton has succeeded also in avoiding the situation found in some community colleges when career education is relegated to second-class status in comparison with liberal studies and transfer programs.

Every teacher hired for the first year was oriented to the comprehensive goals of the institution, including providing programs of study in all areas designated by the state. Specifically, the college sought (1) to provide transfer students with freshman and sophomore courses necessary for transfer; (2) to offer whatever occupational programs were warranted within the community and desired by the students; (3) to design courses and programs of study so that students could enter, leave, and reenter at their own need; (4) to ensure that every student would know the objectives and methods of every course and curriculum and to do everything possible to ensure that each student would achieve at least minimal mastery of courses; (5) to furnish as much "lab" or practical application as possible in every course; (6) to deemphasize learning for grades and to accentuate learning for mastery.

Oakton has abandoned the subject or discipline as a primary basis for organizing faculty and students for administrative purposes. Faculty and students are grouped into four college groups or clusters on the basis of their diversity rather than their similarity. Each group includes twenty-seven or twenty-eight full-time faculty members and about twenty part-time faculty. The heterogeneity of the cluster colleges is indicated by the thirty-five disciplines taught within each of four groups. Group One includes twenty-two disciplines and has one discipline unique to it, anthropology. Group Two includes eighteen disciplines, with four disciplines unique to it. Group Three includes six unique discipline categories out of a total of twenty-one. Group Four includes three unique disciplines out of a total of nineteen. The remaining disciplines are offered by all four clusters or by two or more.

It is the intention of the college to have nearly all subjects available within each cluster. The individual clusters will evolve and develop their own specific identity and uniqueness. During the first year, 1971–72, these differences were considered minimal; there were far more similarities than differences, and the few differences that there were did not form any systematic pattern. Students, prospective students, and outside observers saw more differences than did the staff.

Students were originally assigned to groups in July 1971, on the basis of six factors: high school rank and grade-point average, ACT scores, curriculum choice, age, sex, and whether a new or returning student. All factors except curriculum choice were used to achieve heterogeneity within the cluster group, not homogeneity. Curriculum choice was a segregating factor in those instances where the programs were small, having only one or two teachers. Examples are child care and mechanical technology. Part-time students taking only one course were put into whatever cluster their teacher was in.

Facilitating learning and individualizing instruction are primary goals at Oakton. Within the cluster system a student increasingly has the opportunity to choose the *way* he learns as well as the courses he takes. By using the directory, a student is able, when he registers for a class, to select a section in which a particular known approach to that course will be followed.

Another advantage to the cluster system is the reinforcement of learning through a narrative student-progress report. Within each cluster the teachers have a record of their own students' concurrent courses, and have frequent informal contact with their students' concurrent teachers. All faculty members are encouraged to keep an anecdotal record of student progress and to share this record with other teachers. Out of the records thus accumulated, proposals for revisions of the directory are facilitated.

Faculty have been placed in groups so as to spread among them subject specialties and approaches to teaching, as described in the directory. Each group, for example, has teachers who, regardless of their teaching specialties, have specialized skills in testing. Similarly, each group has at least two student-development faculty members, as well as members with special interests and skills in teaching via auto-tutorial and laboratory-centered methods. In cluster meetings, the focus is constantly upon curriculum development and on teaching approach.

The decision to produce and publish the directory of courses and sections was a natural one, a part of the larger pattern of decisions that has been sketched here. The only barriers were procedural—how to "sell" the concept to faculty who had never done anything like it before, and how to "sell" the expenditure of tax dollars to the board of trustees. The faculty had been prepared for the requirement to write behavioral objectives from the time of the intial preschool orientation in August 1970, when Arthur Cohen of UCLA came to meet with us and discuss some of the concepts underlying both of his then-new books, *Dateline '79* and *Objectives.* The board also had been prepared for something unusual in the way of a catalog or class schedule (we regard the directory as a supplementary publication, reinforcing these two much more traditional documents, one published once a year and the other published each semester or term).

The directory has not had equally enthusiastic and meaningful involvement from all faculty members. It has had contributions, however, from all full-time faculty members whose participation in the instructional program was known far enough in advance to make their contribution possible. Nor has it been unanimously endorsed by the board. Questions remain, but only continued application of the same kind of effort we have been applying since Oakton's beginnings will answer these questions. It is too early to be definitive.

## Evaluation

The directory enhances the educational process at Oakton Community College by facilitating a number of activities that contribute to teaching and learning. At this time the contribution of the directory to these activities is not measurable in output units. Recently, the total college program has been subjected to two institutional self-studies, one in connection with the accreditation process of the North Central Association and the other based upon the standardized procedures of an instrument designed for periodic readministration to determine trends.

The writing and use of behavioral objectives have been facilitated by the existence of the directory, which displays to the student and the nonstudent alike both the strengths and weaknesses of the planning that lies behind every course. The visibility of details about course objectives and procedures enhances accountability even when a strict requirement for behavioral objectives is omitted from the mix. Faculty members and students take more seriously a "contract" in the form of a course outline or syllabus which is available before registration, rather than something that the instructor may devise, duplicate, and distribute "off the cuff" during the first week of class.

The existence of the directory facilitates the advisory process. It gives prospective students and those who are assisting them a basis for making important decisions about personal goals, personal styles of life and learning, the relationships of classes to occupational goals, and the sequence of educational experiences which the student should be seeking. It substitutes elements of depth and seriousness for the unhelpful, arbitrary, and superficial discussion that has characterized much academic advisement.

Peer counseling of new students by older students relies heavily on the directory. After taking several classes taught according to the published description, students are able to offer less experienced students sound advice about faculty members whose classes they have experienced. By relying on instructional details given in the directory, they can similarly advise even about classes and instructors with which they have no first-hand experience. They can help the newcomer to take the registration process seriously.

Reliance on placement tests or the random assignment of individual students to individual classes is being replaced at Oakton by reliance on the directory, for it serves as a selection instrument before the fact. Each student knows his own learning style better than anyone else does, or at least he can get to know his own learning style better than anyone else can know it. Thus, he is his own best advisor-counselor, with the help of peers, professionals, and the directory.

## Prospects

The directory itself, and the bundle of policies and procedures of which it is a part, will evolve as the institution matures. The form and use of the directory are closely related to other innovations at the college, and in fact are not completely separable for purposes of accurate discussion.

One possible future innovation at Oakton is the replacement of traditional nomenclature for four academic ranks (professor, associate professor, assistant professor, instructor), essentially a purely "vertical" system of faculty classification. A new system of identifying titles now under consideration would distinguish among the specialties in method. This innovation also relates closely to the thinking embodied in the directory. As we proceed to differentiate the functions of professionals who are managers of learning, we hope to apply names to the various functions that will differentiate members of the faculty not on the basis of seniority and relative prestige (and salary), but on the basis of how they go about their jobs. New faculty classification nomenclature might include reference to specific faculty responsibilities, such as testing, autotutorial supervision, and coordinating developmental studies. If we move toward a better nomenclature, this nomenclature will be reflected in the directory of courses and sections, and the descriptions will help to make the new nomenclature meaningful, just as the new titles will contribute to the significance of the directory.

## Articulation

Articulation has posed no problems, either within the institution or externally. All four clusters produce and use the directory, and there is no internal element dragging its feet. Externally, we use the traditional college catalog with its more or less standard course descriptions to communicate with registrars and admissions officers. Transcripts are traditional in form and, basically, in content. We have jettisoned E and F grades. Students may pass a course (grades A through D), withdraw voluntarily (grade of W), or continue to work on the course with a grade of X, which means "Student has not yet successfully completed the course." His counselor and his teacher work with him to finish the course; when he does, the X is replaced on the transcript by the earned letter grade ranging from A through D. Any student who can use the directory will find other catalogs simple, but he will have no problem of transfer of training from directory use to conventional catalog use.

## A Model Procedure

As the foregoing sections show, Oakton did not innovate on a single front, or with a single device. The directory of courses and sections is a good beginning, however, for an institution that wants to start with something concrete. A directory approach can be developed by identifying a group of faculty members small enough to be able to work closely together, but diverse enough to assure that there will be variations in their approaches to teaching; setting aside funds for typing, layout, and printing of enough copies of the catalog to serve a significant sample of students each semester for two years; providing opportunities, through in-service training or other means, for all members of the experimental group to learn the process of writing and testing behavioral objectives in their respective disciplines, and to come to common agreement on the content and form of section descriptions; allowing time for the descriptions to be written and edited; composing and publishing the directory with enough lead time to allow full exposure of the finished product to students in the process of registering; reinforcing the importance of the directory both at the beginning and at the end of courses; keeping students aware of the nature of the "contract" and soliciting their comments and criticism on individual descriptions; and recycling the entire process. One useful approach to formative evaluation of directory content is to have students write their own descriptions of the courses they have just taken.

# III

# Developing Noncampus Alternatives

If the creation of innovative colleges such as those described in Chapter Two requires great commitment and tenacity, the creation of even more radical ventures—institutions and agencies that reject major traditions of higher education—requires even more. Such ventures (for instance, a decision to offer instruction in scattered locations with no central campus, or to rely on townspeople rather than professors for the bulk of instruction) not only challenge conventional concepts of academic life but raise questions about their own legitimacy. To what extent are such colleges rightly colleges? How can they be considered truly academic? Are they not by definition inferior?

Throughout the history of American higher education, radical institutions such as the first normal schools, technological schools, land-grant colleges, experimental liberal arts institutions, and the open-door comprehensive community colleges have faced this stigma of illegitimacy and second-class status. During recent years, however, the path of equally radical innovations has been eased somewhat—because of increased acceptance of educational experimentation within American higher education at large; because of support from prestigious foundations, government agencies, and task forces such as the Commission on Non-Traditional Study; and because of the success of such foreign examples as England's Open University.

This chapter describes five educational innovations that depart radically from academic tradition: an external-degree program, two noncampus colleges, a statewide television system, and the venture of a public library into nontraditional study. Perhaps significantly, four of these five stem from basic state government support (augmented by extensive financial help from business and industry or from foundations), and the fifth relies heavily on foundation and association aid. Nonetheless, even with such backing, unconventional efforts such as these face uphill struggles for acceptance. All five of these programs are attempting to use new resources in serving a neglected clientele: adults beyond the traditional college-age years.

Although divergent in their techniques, all five programs contend that their form should follow function: that they need not be bound to conventional definitions of college to be successful—and, indeed, that they must break away from conventional concepts of the campus, the faculty, and even education in order to succeed. All of them emphasize the goal of assessing and certifying the manifest competence of students, but differ on approaches to this end. That the goal is as yet far from being achieved is an impetus to them all.

As these cases illustrate, leadership for nontraditional programs is equally important as for campus-based institutions such as those described in Chapter Two; but even more critical for these clearly unconventional programs is the stamp of legitimacy afforded by state support and by foundation endorsement. Without this legitimacy, these programs could all too readily be dismissed as unacceptable alternatives to campus-based institutions, and as only little better than diploma mills.

How to win the acceptance of the academic community, as well as political and foundation backing, has been a dilemma for each of these institutions. By and large, their tactic has been that of "independence through co-optation": they have retained their autonomous status while encouraging widespread advice from existing institutions. By this action their potentially negative influence was converted to a positive supporting force. For example, New York's CPEP and Regents External Degree programs have depended on the faculties of New York's public and private colleges and universities for continuing advice, for the determination of course and degree standards, and for decisions as to whether particular students should be awarded credit for achievement on specific examinations. This liaison has been a wise move, for it has given existing institutions and their faculty members a feeling of influence over the program and decreased their sense of threat. In fact, the advisory groups of faculty have been pleased enough with the examinations and degree requirements of the new programs that they have permitted great flexibility to the staff in determining how students can meet these requirements, including the transfer of on-campus work from other institutions. Similarly, although the Oklahoma television system has capitalized on the advantages of electronic technology—its capacity to span long distances and to adapt to the time and place needs of adults in business and industry—it illustrates a judicious retention of traditional procedures through faculty control, supervision, and essential "ownership" of self-produced instructional materials, student-faculty interaction, and a clearcut division of institutional mission among the participating colleges and universities—for instance, the offering of developmental education by the community colleges; medical, legal, and engineering education by these particular professional schools; and occupational education by specialized trade and technological schools. Asking faculty members at these institutions to follow their ordinary teaching procedures, the Oklahoma system merely extends their classroom instruction to students remote from the campus.

In the Oklahoma television project, the presence and strength of support from the business and industrial firms with operations remote from the university centers was a special positive force. The Citizens League that helped Minnesota Metropolitan during its formulation stage provided a similar positive influence not attributable to a given individual or change leader. These illustrate a recurrent observation of forces of an extrapersonal kind— namely, group actions, sometimes official and at others informal, which promulgate policies, programs, laws, and the like, bearing in turn significantly on an innovation.

The independent-study project of the Dallas Public Library has similarly been aided by the endorsement of Southern Methodist University. But of all five of the cases, Dallas illustrates more than any other the need not only for academic and financial approval but for determined initiative within a nontraditional project. Rather than stemming from inside the library, initiative came originally from the three outside groups that eventually funded the project: the Council on Library Resources, the National Endowment for the Humanities, and the College Entrance Examination Board. These groups were looking for a test site, and Dallas responded to their initiative. In hindsight the project leaders realized their error in not including librarians from the five branch libraries in the planning process and the development of the proposal for funding. The librarians felt that they were being asked to assume a new role—that of academic counselor—for which they were not prepared, rather than one which merely extended their traditional readers' advisory services; and the library system provided no specific funds for needed supplies, such as extra copies of books on the project reading list. As a result, not only were most of the librarians neutral to the project, rather than advocates of it, but the potential consumers of the service too often found that its publicity exceeded its capacity: the actual operation and follow through were poor.

In short, if dramatically nontraditional approaches to higher education are to succeed, internal determination to achieve high-priority but unfulfilled goals must be combined with helpful external forces that provide financial and academic support.

## DEGREE BY EXAMINATION:
## NEW YORK STATE PROGRAMS

DONALD J. NOLAN, *director, Regents External Degree Program, New York State Education Department*

Each of the two major innovations discussed here is important in its own right, but the two are united under a unique system of education whose legal title is the Regents of the University of the State of New York (USNY). The first innovation is the College Proficiency Examination Program, a series of college-level equivalency tests offered primarily to enable individuals to earn college credit without attending a higher institution. The second major innovation is the Regents External Degree Program, which is the natural culmination of the credit-by-examination system, through which an individual may earn a college degree without any formal classroom attendance.

The University of the State of New York is a comprehensive and unified educational system that encompasses all educational institutions and agencies, public and private, at all levels—including ing museums, libraries, and historical societies. The board of regents —laymen and women elected by the legislature for fifteen-year terms—presides over the university. The regents appoint a commissioner, who serves as president of the university and who directs the state education department, the administrative arm of the board. In addition to determining the state's educational policies and establishing standards for maintaining quality, the regents also have the power to grant degrees (although they have not done so until recently).

Despite their prestige, wide experience, and broad powers, the regents did not venture into direct services in higher education until 1960. They did so then, with the establishment of the College Proficiency Examination Program, only at the urging of a special commission on higher education. Specifically, the board of regents (or the state education department) was asked to sponsor the development of a series of examinations to enable individuals to earn college credit without attending college. In 1970, Commissioner

Ewald B. Nyquist asked the regents to go one step further, proposing that the board award a college degree to anyone who could qualify, with no formal classroom attendance required. The resulting program, known as the Regents External Degree Program, offers an Associate in Arts, an Associate in Applied Science in nursing, and a Bachelor of Arts and a Bachelor of Science in business administration.

## College Proficiency Examination Program

The College Proficiency Examination Program (CPEP) received its initial impetus in the well-known Heald Commission report to the governor and the board of regents in 1960. In this report, entitled "Meeting the Increasing Demand for Higher Education in New York State," the commission (chaired by Henry P. Heald) proposed that "a program be established by the regents which would permit students to acquire regular college credit for their achievements without regular attendance at formal college classes." In 1961 the regents included this recommendation in their proposals for the expansion and improvement of education in New York State, with particular reference to formal requirements for teachers' certification. During the two years that followed, the staff of the state education department arrived at decisions, stemming from advisory board recommendations, about first steps for the proficiency-examination program. The staff decided to prepare the examinations first in mathematics and languages and then in most of the other commonly offered introductory courses. A project director was named, and an advisory board of representatives from public and private institutions was established. The advisory board recommended using on a trial basis certain Advanced Placement examinations of the College Entrance Examination Board, the then newly developed Modern Language Association proficiency tests for teachers and advanced students of foreign languages, and a small number of new examinations to be developed especially for the program. Freshman-level courses not covered by the Advanced Placement testing program and tests to meet teacher certification requirements followed later.

CPEP represented a new approach for New York State's independent learners in the 1960s, one that would eventually be tried nationally by the College Level Examination Program (CLEP). Since 1955, it is true, the Advanced Placement Program of the College Board had offered the opportunity for accelerated high school students to do college-level work while still in secondary school. But in most if not all instances, these students attended formal classes to prepare for the tests, and admission to the examinations was limited to such individuals. CPEP was intended for anyone who felt qualified, and while many reasons were given for taking the examinations, the primary one was to earn college credit.

A critical decision was made in 1966 to develop proficiency examinations in the nursing sciences. The immediate response was phenomenal. Nursing emerged as a natural field for such examinations, and by 1973 more than 18,000 nursing CPEs had been given, resulting in 30,000 credits earned. The success of these efforts in CPEP had much to do with the decision to offer an external degree in nursing.

In 1969, the third director (the present writer) was named. He acted quickly to reinstate the Modern Language Association's proficiency tests, which had been stopped in 1965. By 1970, the stage was set for a dramatic new thrust in New York higher education. In 1970, more CPEs were given than in the entire six-year previous history of CPEP. Ten thousand tests taken by independent learners had resulted in colleges across the state awarding over six thousand credits.

That September Ewald B. Nyquist was inaugurated as commissioner of education and president of the University of the State of New York. He seized that occasion to announce plans for an external degree, a decision which flowed naturally from ten years of experience with CPEP.

CPEP has continued to flourish. Through the summer of 1974, some forty thousand CPEs had resulted in over sixty thousand credits in over forty different subjects.

The decision in the early years of CPEP to leave the matter of awarding credit to the colleges was also critical. Participation in CPEP has remained voluntary; although this decision occasionally resulted in some students being denied credit which independent scholars felt they deserved, in the long run it made the credit-by-examination route available to many more students.

## Regents External Degree Program

Following Commissioner Nyquist's inaugural address in September 1970, when he proposed that the regents award degrees to all who could qualify, Alan Pifer, president of the Carnegie Corporation, addressed the annual meeting of the College Entrance Examination Board in October. "Is it time for an external degree?" asked Pifer, suggesting experimentation on two fronts: a teaching model and an examining model. The challenge was accepted by Commissioner Nyquist and Chancellor Ernest Boyer of the State University of New York (SUNY). Soon four-party conversations were underway involving the state education department, SUNY, the Carnegie Corporation, and the Ford Foundation. Staff members visited many institutions trying related ideas, including the British Open University. Early in 1971 nearly two million dollars in grants were awarded; and work began on establishing the Regents External Degree and SUNY's nonresidential unit, Empire State College (discussed later in this chapter).

During this planning period, the most critical decision was made: that the faculty would play the same fundamental role in the external-degree program as they had in the proficiency examinations. This meant that the faculty committees would establish the degree requirements, determine how these could be met, and recommend to the regents those individuals who were qualified for degrees. A second important decision involved the selection of the first fields of study in which external degrees would be awarded. The field of business appeared to lend itself to the external-degree approach. Large numbers of businessmen are qualified by experience and training to work independently toward a degree, and there are extensive programs of formal and informal education in business and industry which constitute an important, but previously untapped, educational resource. The planners also concluded that a two-year Associate in Arts external degree would be desirable, since it would establish a general education base for the bachelor's degree, whether in business or liberal arts. During the spring of 1971, the director met with key leaders in two-year college education and from schools of business, who recommended several of their colleagues to serve as faculty on the two degree committees. The Associate in Arts faculty, numbering about fifteen, decided upon a fairly traditional pattern of degree requirements but took pride in having introduced considerable flexibility in the ways that students could satisfy them.

The faculty agreed to accept appropriate scores on CPEP, CLEP, Advanced Placement tests, and courses of study and examinations offered by the United States Armed Forces Institute. They also decided to recognize military educational programs with the recommendations of the Commission on Accreditation of Service Experiences of the American Council on Education.

The Associate in Arts faculty also wished to make it possible for students to earn credit by means of special oral, written, or performance examinations, whenever existing tests were not appropriate. Known as "special assessment," this approach is used especially to assess artistic, literary, and musical accomplishments, as well as knowledge or skills gained on the job. Thus far no credit toward an external degree has been earned by special assessment, though the faculty has agreed to permit a student to earn the Associate in Arts entirely by this method.

The baccalaureate degree in business faculty evolved in a slightly different fashion. The ten-man committee framed requirements which included both a general education and a business component. It established five "majors," giving the student the option to elect either accounting, finance, management of human resources, marketing, or operations management.

In the spring of 1972, a registrar's office was established. It handles admissions, ongoing evaluations, the issuance of status reports, and the preparation and presentation of degree candidates' records for consideration by the faculty. It also is responsible for a variety of studies to be carried out on both candidates and graduates, and will continue to conduct longitudinal studies in the future.

In October 1971, Commissioner Nyquist announced plans to add the field of nursing to the external-degree program. From the beginning it was emphasized that the external degree in nursing would not be a substitute for traditional collegiate programs, but rather would serve as another track to a degree for those individuals with the knowledge, motivation, and self-discipline to attempt it. Furthermore, the external degree in nursing would also provide considerable assistance to collegiate programs through the development of a clinical performance assessment instrument.

The nursing faculty committee chose as its first degree program the Associate in Applied Science in nursing, with the understanding that if this program were successful and if sufficient funds were available, the idea of an external Bachelor of Science degree would also be explored.

As the Carnegie-Ford grants, totaling $800,000, began to run out, new funds were sought. In March 1973, the Kellogg Foundation gave the Regents $528,000 to continue the development of the external degree in nursing, while the Carnegie Corporation made a second grant of $300,000 to complete work on the Associate in Arts and the baccalaureate in business, and to prepare the fourth Regents External Degree, the Bachelor of Arts. A faculty committee for the external A.B. was selected in the fall of 1973.

From the very outset of the external-degree program, emphasis was placed upon securing a broad range of advice and guidance. The advisory board on Regents External Degrees numbers among its members college and bank presidents, a national program director, graduate and undergraduate students, and the education director from a major corporation.

At the same time, it was felt that the faculty had to do more than establish degree requirements and develop examinations. They had to be a faculty with a high degree of visibility, not only that which comes from attaining recognition in one's field but visibility in the sense that they had to stand publicly behind the degree programs they created.

One group of potential students was singled out by the staff as deserving of special recruitment efforts: men and women in the armed services. With the advent of the all-volunteer services, the Defense Department was increasing its emphasis upon higher education and the possession of degrees. Because of the highly mobile nature of the military, the Defense Department was looking for flexible degree programs, with minimal residence requirements, and in which recognition would be given to previous study, both in colleges and through military schools and USAFI. The Regents External Degree Program met all these conditions and then some. Of the first 727 graduates of the Associate in Arts program, 418 were members of the armed services.

## Productivity and Evaluation

An evaluation of the effectiveness of the Regents External Degree Program is now underway through a series of studies conducted by the program staff itself and through outside accrediting agencies. The Middle States Association of Colleges and Secondary Schools has granted candidate status to the program, and preliminary discussions have been held with the National League for Nursing and the American Assembly of Collegiate Schools of Business.

The several staff analyses prepared thus far reveal to some extent the nature of the external-degree candidate and graduate. Through 1974 more than 7500 students from all fifty states and several foreign countries had enrolled: more than 4000 in the Associate in Arts program, more than 1600 in business administration, and more than 1600 in nursing. Graduates of the Associate in Arts program numbered more than 2000. Over 300 students were in baccalaureate programs, which started in June 1974 and from which eleven had graduated. Fifty-four percent of the graduates are now enrolled in a postsecondary educational program. Seventy-nine percent of these graduates received full credit for their external Associate in Arts degree.

It is doubtful whether the regents' program of external degrees and proficiency examinations will or ought to be duplicated elsewhere. The strength of any approach, however, which attempts to experiment with the New York external-degree model, will lie with strong faculty involvement, from as many colleges and universities as possible. Without such full participation, the project will have little prospect of success.

## ALTERNATIVE LEARNING-CREDENTIALING MODEL: EMPIRE STATE COLLEGE

JAMES W. HALL, *president, Empire State College of SUNY*

Jo Fictitious, thirty-eight years old, urban blue-collar worker, father of five, is a housewife and bachelor archeologist living in the suburbs who as a retired grandmother has just graduated from high school at age sixteen. Jo is less fictitious than composite or indicative of the spectrum of students that Empire State College, in Saratoga Springs, New York, was created to serve. Empire State College believes that education is not confined to the walls of a classroom and that people learn and require education throughout their lives. Because the traditional college model, with its fixed curriculum and requirements of time and place, made higher education remote or inaccessible to many students, the State University of New York created Empire State College as an alternative vehicle. Within the framework of Empire State College, students have the flexibility to design—with faculty counsel—individual degree programs (including independent study, tutorials, experiences present and past, classrooms, and seminars) responsive to their needs and interests. Students progress at a pace determined by their capabilities and the weight of other responsibilities. It is this flexibility—in programs of study and scheduling arrangements—that is the heart of the Empire State College experience. The college has no campus and offers no formal courses. One of the five regional centers also serves as the center for coordinating the network of learning centers that will eventually touch all areas of the state, with satellites in easy commuting distance of every citizen. The college offers baccalaureate- and associate-degree programs and is open to all persons who can benefit from these alternative approaches.

Empire State College was a result of social pressures for a form of quality higher education that would (1) provide access to students who require flexibility in time, place, and method of learning; (2) provide content responsive to individual needs and changing social requirements; and (3) seek to find more cost-effective patterns of delivery. This new institution was founded by State

University of New York in response to significant changes in American society and as a result of reexamination of some of the basic premises on which our colleges and universities have operated. The creation of Empire State College, in the spring of 1971, as an alternative "delivery system" solely to replicate a traditional education would not have been a sufficient response. Social realities require that the nontraditional institution move in two directions: toward finding alternative procedures by which traditional content can be made available and evaluated, and simultaneously toward finding ways to redefine the content of that education, so that higher education can better serve diverse students. Rising costs of higher education also make essential an exploration of effective alternative patterns that might cost less than established programs.

### Creation and Implementation

During the late 1960s these assumptions about the existing pattern of higher education were analyzed by several State University of New York panels and university-wide study groups. In the fall of 1970, a planning task force was appointed by Chancellor Ernest L. Boyer to determine how the State University of New York could best meet the new societal needs. On January 27, 1971, he addressed a memo to the trustees, describing the directions and impact of such reexamination: "Every basic assumption on which we've built in the past is being sharply challenged. We must now develop a higher-learning system that is not restricted to a rigid curriculum, a single campus, or a fixed calendar. The new system must be geared to a pattern of offerings which permits each student to study what he wants, when he wants it, and at a place convenient to him."

By the 1970s higher education, after two decades of unprecedented prosperity, was retrenching everywhere. Empire State was seen as an answer to the pressures of individual attention and reduced costs. It would provide a new type of education, focused on student needs. There would be a more personal and intensive faculty-student relationship, with a mentor seeing the students once or twice a month or so. Well-designed independent-study programs would also permit faculty members to deal with substantial numbers of students pursuing individually tailored programs. Faculty would be chosen for their commitment to teaching, their intellectual competencies, and their academic planning and advisement capabilities.

February 1971 also brought the announcement that the Ford Foundation and the Carnegie Corporation would grant $500,000 each to New York State's new nonresidential program (Empire State College). Both foundations had long assisted reform in higher education, and the chancellor's office had maintained contact with them through the course of the planning period.

Empire State opened two learning centers in the fall of 1971. Plans called for the college to have four learning centers, plus the coordinating center at Saratoga Springs, operating by the fall of 1972. This meant that a full staff had to be recruited for each learning center. The staff faced other formidable challenges. An admissions procedure, based on new and broad criteria, was created to serve students of all ages. A tuition and financial-aid structure was designed and geared to an open-term, nonsemester academic plan with flexibility for each student. New kinds of records and transcripts were devised in order to describe adequately the evaluation of a student's learning contracts. The new college had to be linked with a statewide purchasing and accounting system. It had to develop contracts and close relationships with a wide variety of regional organizations and institutions (some of them competitors, and all beset with their own problems). Field-study arrangements were made on a statewide and an international basis. A statewide communications network and media operation was planned and launched. Decisions had to be made on the location of the first learning centers; space had to be located and rented. Publicity explaining the new college had to be available in areas as complex as New York City and as remote as upstate rural hamlets.

### Structure

A number of alternative approaches to the traditional classroom/seminar approach are described in the Empire State College Master Plan. Basic to all approaches is the individually tailored study program prepared between a student and a faculty *mentor;* the mentor helps the student define his goals and plan a program of study and evaluates the student's progress. In the *program mode,* students may select from a wide range of faculty prepared independent study materials and media, providing highly flexible sequences of study. Another alternative recognizes *field studies* or *experiential* aspects of learning, gained through job or life experience, travel, international studies, internships, and the like. The *degree-by-examination* alternative offered by the New York State regents (discussed earlier in this chapter) may be incorporated into students' degree plans at Empire State College; conversely, students who develop competencies through studies undertaken at Empire State College can apply the credit earned toward a Regents External Degree. Finally, Empire State College will offer yet another alternative—the SUNY degree. This is actually a composite or regional degree program in which a student completes a degree at several different institutions. ESC becomes the mechanism which recommends the student to the SUNY board of trustees for a degree.

These alternatives are blended by the learning "contract" or study plan. The contract is an individual study plan which provides both rigor and clarity to the student and at the same time enables the college to maintain academic and fiscal accountability.

## Key Issues

The problems encountered fall into four broad areas: academic programs, governance, credit for life experience, and management and accountability.

*Academic programs.* The most challenging and perplexing problems faced by Empire State College have to do with the important questions of academic quality and program. The shift in emphasis from institutional requirements to student initiatives makes academic issues at Empire State College especially complex. We soon discovered that the design of academic programs in which the student had a significant initiative and control would raise many hard questions. The result was that the staff operated both inductively and deductively. During the first year, students and mentors together created hundreds of contracts, which are each part of larger programs of study. As students have moved from one contract to another, they began to assemble rich and significant programs of study unique to themselves but also responsive to the social contexts in which the programs were created.

The major difference, then, in curriculum development is that—unlike external-degree programs which have hypothesized a standard curriculum and then created learning materials and examinations to enable the student to pursue and demonstrate competency in that program—Empire State College has undertaken the complex task of redefining the meaning and substance of a college degree. When this is done under responsible faculty direction, one can demand high standards of quality or performance in whatever subject matter the student pursues. More important, the student, through participation in the evaluative processes, develops the critical skills necessary to make continuing judgments about quality after the college work is done.

*Governance.* Few issues compare with governance in the attention attracted in recent years among faculty, administrators, and other supporting bodies such as trustees and legislators. Whatever the form found in practice, governance is often a major stumbling block to institutional change. While college faculties have always endorsed the principle of *knowledge change* based upon research findings (although there may be significant time lag between institutions), in matters of *organizational change* faculties have been notoriously conservative. Many an innovative faculty idea has been compromised to death by the numerous faculty committees that commonly are a part of collegiate governance. The reason for creation of separate nontraditional colleges and programs in recent years has been to give such ideas an opportunity to be tested and implemented without the delays and compromises that traditional governance would require. This is one reason that Empire State College was created as a separate body with its own faculty and administration.

Yet Empire State College is not completely free to develop its program entirely as its faculty and administration determine. For one thing, it is committed to developing programs in response to student needs and initiatives. Second, the college has been mandated by the state university to undertake a number of alternative approaches to higher education—and this within a demanding cost framework. The college is not free to develop one alternative to the exclusion of others. Finally, the college is designed to respond to a number of interinstitutional developments (such as a SUNY-wide degree), many of which involve the rights and prerogatives of faculty at other campuses. Clearly, then, the faculty at Empire State College cannot maintain independent substantive programmatic control. An innovative governance framework needs to be created which ensures open discussion, responsiveness to these conditions of systemwide university relationships, and responsible acceptance of change.

For some, the position just suggested may seem an abrogation of the traditional faculty role in collegial governance. Others argue that the faculty can and must maintain responsibility for defining the quality of student performance in whatever alternative or program a student pursues through Empire State College. In many respects, this purpose for the faculty is the most basic and fundamental role of any faculty, but designing a governance format which will recognize it at ESC is proving to be a complex matter.

*Credit for educational life experience.* A third problem area involves the issue of granting college credit for life experience. Most colleges avoid facing this problem by sharply limiting the amount of credit, if any, which can be awarded for nontraditional learning. The truly astonishing fact is that in twenty-five years of the greatest expansion and support ever known in the history of education, a single model which serves a particular body of students has been replicated again and again throughout the nation. This model is insufficient to serve the nontraditional student. Many potential students—including minorities, women, the physically handicapped, prisoners, and working adults generally—confront established curricula which do not relate well to their needs in terms of scheduling, content, or degree aspiration. This means, inescapably, that the college must give greater attention to individual learning and must develop qualitatively sound, flexible, and inclusive assessment procedures which measure the learning through life experience brought by each individual.

*Management and accountability.* Overall management and accountability are especially complex for a statewide college which places diverse learning resources at the student's disposal. While the coordinating center administration maintains overall planning and administrative and fiscal responsibility, a regional structure provides

an operating basis for developing strong interinstitutional relationships and logistical management for students. Each regional center
is headed by a dean. The dean is truly a regional administrator,
responsible for the academic leadership of the students and faculty
(mentors) working with Empire State College in that region, and
for the encouragement of a wide variety of specialized learning opportunities at institutions and agencies in the region. Since only
*mentors* may sign student contracts, they maintain quality control
over the wide range of learning resources engaged by students.

## Costs and Productivity

From the outset, it has been essential for the college to devise
effective alternatives which have the potential for increasing productivity and reducing per-student costs. Empire State College enrollment at the end of the 1974 fiscal year (March 31, 1974) was
1675 full-time equivalents (approximately 2120 students). Costs
for the first three budgets are shown in Table 1.

*Table 1.*

| Expenses | Year | Average Annual Student FTE | Total Cost per Student |
|---|---|---|---|
| $   827,000 | 1971–72 | 105 | $7876 |
| 2,460,000 | 1972–73 | 893 | 2754 |
| 3,847,000 | 1973–74 | 1675 | 2296 |
| 5,059,000 | 1974–75 (projected) | 2806 | 1803 |

## Evaluation and Research

Empire State College has initiated a comprehensive research
and evaluation effort designed to focus on cost-effectiveness analysis. Research will match educational outcomes to financial outlays
for various teaching/learning activities. Essential to success is that
findings and conclusions be used to formulate a systematic program

which is an improvement over the existing one and preserves the nontraditional character of the institution. Only in this way can the experiences of the college be useful throughout the higher education community. The research on the many issues under examination will provide a solid data foundation upon which educational and fiscal decisions can be intelligently based. Empire State College expects its framework for decision making to be as innovative as its academic program. Results of research are now made available to other institutions regularly through publications of the research office.

## COMMUNITY AS CAMPUS:
## MINNESOTA METROPOLITAN STATE COLLEGE

DOUGLAS R. MOORE, *president, Mankato State College; formerly executive vice-president and dean, Minnesota Metropolitan State College*

The chancellor of the Minnesota state college system, G. Theodore Mitau, first advocated the establishment of a seventh state college to serve the Twin Cities metropolitan area in 1968. The Minnesota state college board supported the chancellor's request to include the creation of such a college in the board's legislative program in 1969 (when it was not acted upon by the legislature) and again in 1971. The Minnesota Higher Education Coordinating Commission endorsed the proposal prior to the 1971 session of the legislature, as did the presidents of the existing state colleges and the presidents of the six state junior colleges in the metropolitan area.

From the beginning, Chancellor Mitau and the members of the state college board looked upon the proposed new college as an institution that would provide innovative alternatives in urban higher education. This institution, they said, would devote itself to transfer students from metropolitan junior colleges and area vocational-technical schools, and other adults who needed upper-division educational opportunities to complete degrees. And it would do this not by duplicating efforts of existing institutions but by utilizing new teaching-learning methods.

During the fall of 1970 and the winter of 1971, the issues surrounding the establishment of the college were examined by a committee on higher education formed by the Citizens League, a widely respected civic organization consisting of several hundred Twin Cities metropolitan-area citizens. It has studied and made recommendations on a number of basic issues confronting this metropolitan area, including studies which resulted in the formation of the Metropolitan Council, hailed nationally as a model for metropolitan government. In the spring of 1971, while the legislature was considering Chancellor Mitau's proposal, the Citizens League issued an influential report, *"An Urban College: New Kinds of 'Students' on a New Kind of 'Campus,'"* calling for the creation of Minnesota Metropolitan State College (MMSC). This report had great impact upon the legislature, and most if not all of its recommendations are incorporated into the college.

On May 22, 1971, the legislature—on the basis of local and national needs which it had anticipated when it called upon the HECC to study the question and which had been documented by Chancellor Mitau, the Citizens League, the Carnegie Commission, and the Newman Task Force—authorized the state college board to establish MMSC. Three hundred thousand dollars were appropriated for planning and operating the college during the two fiscal years beginning July 1, 1971, and ending June 30, 1973. The governor signed this bill on June 7, 1971. On June 28, 1971, the state college board, on the recommendation of the chancellor, appointed David E. Sweet as the college's founding president. He had served during the preceding two years as the state college system's vice-chancellor for academic affairs.

At this time of his appointment, the new president was given this charge by Chancellor Mitau: to create a new, innovative, nontraditional college; to emphasize teaching and not research; to utilize all available resources and facilities; to develop a flexible, year-round calendar; and to utilize the specialized experience and expertise of professional men and women within the community.

President Sweet immediately began to gather the nucleus of a staff for the new college. On September 1, 1971, he employed Douglas R. Moore as vice-president and dean and John Cardozo, a local business executive, as secretary-treasurer. A small core of other staff were added later in September. This included three faculty members transferred from the existing state colleges whose salaries were paid by their respective institutions for the first three months. Three additional faculty were added at the same time, and this small staff began planning the college program and operation. In addition to planning, the principal officers of the college set about to raise funds with which to supplement the legislative appropriation. Approximately $800,000 was raised in the next eighteen months from a variety of sources, including the U.S. Office of Education, the Carnegie Corporation, the Hill Family Foundation, and the Bush Foundation.

## Basic Tenets

Four basic tenets define Minnesota Metropolitan State College: (1) The student has authority over and responsibility for his own education. He should be able to design, implement, pay for, and accept the consequences of the educational plan best suited to his individual needs. Obviously, good advice, counsel, and reasoned judgment should be components. (2) The college is completely competence-based in its evaluation of students. Learners are not rewarded (or punished) for an experience or a series of experiences. They are evaluated on the results of the experience—their reflection upon and integration of it as manifest in knowledge, skill, understanding, and attitudes. Demonstrable evidence that the student knows and can do something is the sole criterion for "credit" or certification. (3) The college is oriented to its environment, which is urban. Therefore, what is taught and what is learned is shot through with an urban emphasis. (4) The college is committed to an inventory, integration, and utilization of existing community learning resources. One of the major tasks of the college is to discover, inventory, and disseminate information about the community (the seven-county metropolitan area including Minneapolis and St. Paul).

## Developmental Framework

The implementation of these tenets and the accomplishment of these major tasks are carried out by a coordinating center, a core of full-time staff (professional and support staff), an Office of Learning Development, and an Office of Learning Resources.

The coordinating center houses all full-time staff responsible for program and staff development, records, and processes; dissemination of information; and the general integration, coordination, and management of the college. No classes or courses are scheduled in this facility. A series of satellite centers are projected for the next two years in order to decentralize functions better served by geographical considerations.

The core staff consists largely of professionally trained faculty and administrators who have experience in and commitment to innovative education.

The format for learning development is the single requirement at the college. Each student, with advice and counsel, designs his own program (pact), which is a contract with the institution. The content of the pact is not uniform for all; each student is required however to go through the standard format or process. The Office of Learning Development focuses on process—the procedures involved in educational planning and evaluation. The Office of Learning Resources focuses on the content of education—discovering, identifying, organizing, and delivering persons, places, and events which make the learning possible; in short, the implementation of educational plans and goals.

The most exciting and most frustrating of all community resources MMSC has utilized has been the people. The college has both a full-time and a community faculty. The tasks of the full-time faculty are to plan, to facilitate, to coordinate and to assure continuity. The task of the community faculty is to provide diversity in implementation. The recruitment, screening, and use of a community faculty has been central to the planning and development of the college from its inception. With the earliest news stories about the college came responses which indicated a wide range of interest and large numbers available—from a dairy farmer without a college degree who had studied Latin on his own for forty years to the numerous Ph.D.s employed by industries in the community. A main problem encountered in the use of community faculty is that, to a large extent, their only frame of reference for functioning as a "teacher" is usually a very traditional institutional model with required courses, required attendance, lectures, examinations, and a grading scale from A to F. Another large problem is equity of pay scale. The tension between fiscal constraints and commitment to a fair and appropriate rate of remuneration for both full-time and community faculty is a constant difficulty.

## Productivity

The college admitted its first fifty students on February 1, 1972. Since the college operates without fixed semesters or quarters, it has continued to admit students on a monthly basis. On February 1, 1973, the college graduated its first twelve students. As of June 30, 1974, approximately 950 students were enrolled, and the college had granted degrees to over one hundred. Since the institution is so new, the results of other, more extensive measures of productivity now being applied are not yet available.

## TALKBACK TELEVISION: OKLAHOMA STATE REGENTS FOR HIGHER EDUCATION

E. T. DUNLAP, *chancellor, Oklahoma State Regents for Higher Education*

In February 1970, the Oklahoma legislature authorized and directed the Oklahoma State Regents for Higher Education to establish, maintain, and operate a statewide system of closed-circuit microwave television to extend higher education to the people in all parts of the state. The legislation carried an appropriation to underwrite two thirds of the initial installation costs of the system, and business and industrial establishments of the state were to provide the other one third. The law also provided funds to operate the system in its first year.

The state regents were directed to plan a complete and statewide expansion of the system to all colleges, including junior colleges and technical institutes, both public and private, to establish a complete network of closed-circuit microwave communication whereby the strongest program of postsecondary education offered at any one institution of higher education could be made available to students of all institutions.* A specific purpose of the system as stated in the law was to extend graduate education program opportunities from colleges and universities to employees of businesses and industries at remote locations from campuses. The plan intended that there be a free exchange of credits among institutions in order that an individual could complete all degree requirements utilizing educational experiences of his choice from the strongest teachers available at the various institutions.

The Talkback Television System (TBT), as it is commonly known, simply is an expansion of the college classroom to include students at remote locations for sharing in the classroom instructional activities as they take place. Students receive residence credit and may complete all of the course work required for a degree by attending classes via the TBT system.

Although a number of other universities have established televised-instruction systems, the Oklahoma System is the first statewide, all-institutions (universities, colleges, junior colleges, and technical institutes) system to be installed anywhere.

## Developmental History and Articulation

The initial televised-instruction network linked the University of Oklahoma at Norman, Oklahoma State University at Stillwater, and the University of Tulsa at Tulsa with remote classrooms located at Continental Oil Company at Ponca City, Halliburton Services at Duncan, Kerr-McGee Corporation at Oklahoma City, Phillips Petroleum Company at Bartlesville, Phillips University at Enid, Muskogee Veterans Hospital at Muskogee, the Oklahoma Bureau of Mines at Bartlesville, the Vocational-Technical Center at Ardmore, Oklahoma Christian College at Oklahoma City, Oral Roberts University at Tulsa, Central State University at Edmond, and Oscar Rose Junior College at Midwest City. The network initially had transmitting studios at the University of Oklahoma, Oklahoma State University, and Tulsa University; receiving classrooms at all other locations, with a backbone microwave link going both ways between the University of Oklahoma, Oklahoma State Uni-

---

* This statement deals only with the academic and organizational issues encountered in developing the system. Technical engineering details can be obtained from the regents.

versity, and Tulsa University, and two microwave channels branching from the backbone to all other cities; and instructional-television fixed-service units in Oklahoma City, Tulsa, and Bartlesville.

The network became fully operative in September of 1971. The student-credit-hour production was 833 for the first full year of operation and 2064 for the second year. Virtually all of these credits were at the graduate level in engineering, business, and chemistry.

Participating businesses and industries provide completely furnished and equipped remote classrooms, share with the state the capital costs for installation of the system, and pay for the basic expenses of operation.

An academic policy advisory committee advises and consults with the state regents' staff concerning academic policies and procedures relating to televised instruction. The committee is representative of each of the graduate centers and the state regents' staff.

Studio classrooms are designed for regular campus instruction; at the same time, they provide accommodations for instruction to remote locations via television. Questions or remarks from students in remote classrooms are heard by the professor and by all other students taking the class at the various locations. The professor can call on any student to recite, to respond to a question, or to take part in a discussion by addressing the student by name. This arrangement encourages the continuation of normal classroom procedures and enables a professor to continue teaching in his accustomed manner.

Receiving classrooms are in all other respects regular classrooms. Library facilities available at any of the institutions are available to all students registered for credit in this program, regardless of which institution is offering the specific course. A courier service is provided for the exchange of homework, examinations, references, and other written materials between and among the classrooms of the system on a daily basis.

## Expansion

In *Phase-I* expansion, various receiving and transmitting studios were located and became operational in September 1972. These studios link several institutions for the purpose of providing additional programs—among them, programs in health fields and special programs for the disadvantaged.

*Phase-II* expansion called for connections to extend from the Oklahoma City headquarters to fifteen institutions in southeast Oklahoma, terminating in the extreme southeast corner of the state in the Poteau-Hodgins area. Included were public and private colleges, correctional institutions, model-city program centers, and vocational centers. This phase of the expansion made it possible to expand the plan beyond the fifteen centers originally included.

*Phase-III* expansion supplemented the microwave system already established. It projected nearly two dozen locations to be added to the system in high schools, military bases, hospitals, and governmental offices, as well as in other postsecondary institutions. The expansion of the network allowed the addition not only of the locations selected but of any other that might be situated in the path of the microwave system. Envisioned in this expansion were five transmitting studios as well as a fixed-service channel and added microwave channels.

*Phase-IV* expansion moved to include the addition of seven receiving locations because other agencies, businesses, and industries were expected to request permission to tie into the system during this phase.

*Phase-V* expansion looked to an additional six institutions which were expected to have televised-instruction receiving classrooms available in the near future.

Estimated capital funding is provided as follows: the state, $3,270,500 (62 percent); the federal government, $1,055,000 (20 percent); private industry, $633,000 (12 percent); and institutions, $316,500 (6 percent).

## Critical Decisions

Several factors were important to the successful establishment of the Oklahoma Higher Education Televised Instruction System during its initial phase of development.

Early decisions on several matters helped administrators and faculty members to be more accepting of the program than they may ordinarily have been. Only regular faculty who volunteer teach courses via the system, and they do not receive extra pay for such teaching. (In spite of the dire predictions of several administrators and faculty members, today more faculty desire to teach than the System can accommodate.)

To assure the quality of instruction offered via the System, adequate reference materials are provided at each receiving classroom location, students are in the classroom studio with the teacher for all courses offered, and classes are not taped except for make-up sessions.

As the program was being developed, it became evident that the System would not work unless institutions established liberal transfer of credit policies. Therefore, institutional policies were modified to enable a student to transfer up to half the credits earned via the System from other institutions to the institution where the student expected to earn a degree.

Another problem resolved early was that students at remote locations wanting to enroll in courses being taught via the System were being asked to go through the same registration process as on-campus students. This process involved trips to the campus for tests and physical examinations. When this problem was brought to the attention of the Academic Planning Committee, the process was streamlined so that students could enroll for courses via the System at the receiving classroom location.

The efforts of the Academic Advisory Committee relative to the televised-instruction system have improved articulation between institutions. Term beginning and ending dates and vacation periods have become more uniform. Several institutions are no longer offering courses on their campus, but their students receive the courses they need via the televised-instruction system. Other institutions have divided the courses to be offered for a particular degree program and thus free faculty for other activities such as research and program development. Team teaching, with faculty from three institutions sharing in the instruction of a class, has been accomplished. The offering of certain courses on alternate years by cooperating institutions has reduced duplication of effort in several instances.

Articulation within institutions has also improved. Interdisciplinary seminars and special programs for correctional personnel and inmates offered via the system have enabled individuals from several departments to plan and work together.

## Productivity

The televised-instruction system has grown steadily since operations began in the fall of 1971. The number of student credit hours produced in 1972–73 was more than double that of 1971–72. Courses offered via the system now include undergraduate as well as graduate courses, and the kinds of seminars offered are more varied. As already noted, student-credit-hour production had exceeded 2000 by the second year of operation. Community requests for televised instruction have constantly exceeded the state regents' ability to expand the system. While at first courses were provided mainly for industrial personnel, other groups are now being served: on-campus students who want to take courses at other institutions, correctional personnel, personnel stationed at military bases, and a variety of other groups.

## Future Directions

A state regents' study, completed in December 1969, which called for the immediate establishment of a televised-instruction system, also recommended that the microwave system developed for television be able to handle data transmission as well. A statewide computer network is envisioned. Oklahoma institutions are planning to share their Computer Assisted Instruction (CAI) programs and to obtain programs from throughout the country. The computer network would also be used for exchanging library information between institutions and for training students in computer science and would provide all institutions of higher education in the state with the computer capabilities they need for administration and research. The possibility of linking the state regents' televised-instruction system to community cable systems also is being explored. (For a summary of cable TV developments, see Cabinet Committee on Cable Communications, 1974.)

## Procedural Recommendations

A brief guide for establishing and operating a televised instruction system such as the one described here would include the following steps: (1) Have sound reasons for establishing the system.

(2) Involve educational leaders in a long-range study of immediate and future needs. (3) Develop general policies, guidelines, and estimates of capital and operational costs before trying to sell the program to industry, legislators, faculty, and others. (4) Employ a director with educational background for the program as soon as possible; the director should then employ a chief engineer with microwave experience before moving forward with implementation plans. (5) Allow at least twelve months for establishing the network. (6) Develop administrative and operational details concurrent with the installation of the electronic equipment, which saves developmental time and resources. (7) Be open to suggestions for improving the operation of the program from those involved. (8) Maintain maximum flexibility in handling suggestions for course offerings and their initiation in the system. (9) Be willing to offer seminars and short courses when regular courses are not scheduled. (10) Review policies and guidelines periodically and establish specific evaluation machinery.

## INVOLVEMENT OF A PUBLIC LIBRARY IN HIGHER EDUCATION: DALLAS PUBLIC LIBRARY

DAVID L. REICH, *chief librarian, Chicago Public Library; formerly deputy director, Dallas Public Library*

With its foundation-funded Independent Study Project, the Dallas Public Library (DPL) was given an opportunity to test a nontraditional approach to learning at the higher education level. The Independent Study Project began in September 1971, when the doors of five branch libraries in Dallas opened with a new service to the citizens of the area: a service providing direct assistance to adults who want to study independently and to obtain academic recognition for their learning.

### Time Frame

The real beginning for the DPL Independent Study Project (ISP) was in January 1970, when the library was visited by representatives of the College Entrance Examination Board (CEEB), the National Endowment for the Humanities (NEH), and the Council on Library Resources (CLR). The meeting, which had been arranged by the CLR, was to introduce the library to the College Level Examination Program (CLEP) and to the idea of a project in which the library would serve as a center for CLEP information and materials and for providing assistance to CLEP candidates. After considerable study, the library affirmed interest in the idea and began designing an appropriate project—namely, a project whereby the library would serve as a CLEP information and assistance center and, further, as an assistance center for adults who could be attracted to independent learning, not only for learning that could lead to CLEP but learning of a personal sort directed to self-enrichment. Since CLEP is not another type of formal education, the Independent Study Project would not be in competition with the local colleges and universities for students; the library, instead, should help direct students to those institutions. CLR, NEH, and CEEB offered encouragement and expressed enthusiasm as the proposal went through numerous drafts. Southern Methodist University (SMU) also offered its support and eventually even offered to participate in the project.

In January 1971, a formal proposal was submitted to the Council of Library Resources, who forwarded it to the National Endowment for the Humanities. In June 1971, the library was notified that the project was funded for a total of $100,000 ($50,000 from the NEH, and $25,000 each from the CLR and the CEEB). The two-year project was instituted in September 1971. Five of the Dallas Public Library's fourteen branches were selected to participate in the project.

### Decisions and Barriers

An initial problem for the library was how to relate its new service for adults to existing college opportunities in the area. The library did not want to encourage adults to prepare for CLEP examinations if there were no schools locally where they could go to obtain credit via CLEP examinations for what they had learned. In January 1970, only a limited number of programs for accepting

CLEP existed in the colleges and universities in Dallas and north central Texas. At that time, a CEEB staff member from the board's regional office in Austin was visiting the academic institutions in the area, working with them toward the end that the schools would develop programs for accepting CLEP for credit. The August 1972 monthly report of the project director announced, "The year's end finds credits for two years of college easily available at almost all area colleges, with twelve hours available at all campuses of the Dallas County Community College."

One decision which was not made and which should have been made was to involve service librarians in the design of the project. Instead, the proposal was prepared by a team of members of the library's administrative staff. Possibly as a result, the on-the-line service librarians have tended to view the project (and the service) as something extra from their regular services. If they had been involved in the project earlier—as early as the actual designing of the program—their attitude toward it might have been somewhat more enthusiastic.

Another problem arose with the suggestion of grant funding for the project. The library, as a department of the city of Dallas, is subject to budgetary, auditing, and personnel control by the city; that fact necessitated lengthy discussions with city administrators in order to reconcile the requirements of the city concerning the handling of grants and those of the principal funder, the National Endowment for the Humanities.

Another difficulty that developed during the first few months of the project had to do with attracting adults to use this new service. The library had understood from the beginning that it would have to recruit adults in the community to become independent students. Therefore, for recruitment purposes, the project's advisory committee decided to use the project's contingency fund to purchase half-page advertisements (with coupons to be mailed in) in the local newspaper's special education issues. These advertisements did bring considerable response, except that the same half-page ad in Spanish in a local Spanish-American paper brought no response at all. The advisory committee felt, however, that special advertising funds should have been built into the project's budget.

An early decision to hire a professional educator from the

education field for the project director was changed in the middle of the preparation of the Project's proposal. It was felt initially that an educator would bring to the project a particular expertise that would be needed. However, after Southern Methodist University became a participant in the program, it was felt that SMU would provide the ISP with the education expertise and that, therefore, the project director could be a professional librarian with an appropriate background in service to adults.

**Delivering the Service**

Preparing the library for the project and preparing for the actual delivery of the services promised by ISP meant facing new challenges, particularly in conveying the concept of ISP and CLEP to librarians and to SMU faculty members. The reaction of the librarians was not at all as enthusiastic as those who had worked on the ISP proposal had hoped it would be, probably because the librarians were all graduates of traditional library schools, which do not typically stress counseling of individuals who are seeking college credit by nonconventional paths. Nonetheless, the enthusiasm of the librarians grew considerably with the progress of the actual service. The SMU faculty who were to prepare the study guides and reading lists for ISP had to be convinced also—particularly since these study guides and reading lists required a nontraditional approach, and these instructors had traditional backgrounds. Those were neither clear nor easy assignments to the somewhat traditional college instructors. Many of them responded initially by hurrying to look at the CLEP examinations with the idea of designing their study guides and reading lists to fit the examinations.

Should the library change so that librarians will serve as counselors to independent students in the library? Or should the cooperating colleges and universities change so that their counselors could go out from campus to the libraries? These are questions that will have to be answered finally in other studies and projects. The Independent Study Project has demonstrated that adults who want to learn independently and gain academic credit by examination want and need considerable guidance, counseling, and reassurance—more than the librarians in the five DPL branches have been able to provide.

## Future of the Project

After the first year of ISP, it was clear that the small number of persons attracted as ongoing independent students could not justify fiscal support for the program. Staff dedicated to the full-time coordination of such a program, frequent mailings of newsletters to maintain the interest of the students, and the printing of the newsletters would require no little amount of funds. Anticipating that it may have to find a broader support base, the library has been working with the Dallas County Community College District to design cooperative programs of service, whereby the library can continue to offer to the citizens information on and assistance in various options for learning.

Aside from serving the independent student as a resource for information about the educational options available to him in his community, the library might continue its active role of providing for direct assistance to the student as it has done in ISP. As the project was designed, however, the program offered something *so* unstructured that it might have been *too* unstructured for many people. Perhaps the library, while still providing approaches to unstructured independent study, should offer, in the same setting, independent study with some structure.

Some who have viewed the Independent Study Project from a distance suggest that the library might become the true open university: "a college that is a library, and a library that is a college" (Shores, 1968). Perhaps it is time now for public libraries to become not competitors but partners with academic institutions in higher education. The Dallas Public Library's Independent Study Project might best be viewed as an early contract in the partnership between academic institutions and the public library.

## How to Become an Independent-Study Center

Other public libraries may be interested in developing a similar cooperative program of service with colleges in their own communities. The following steps, based on the DPL experience, are suggested: (1) Work with library staff to develop program goals related to higher education opportunities. (2) Investigate the community to determine what is available in the way of nontraditional options, particularly credit-by-examination programs of the local colleges and universities, for those adults interested in independent study. (3) Explore possibilities of cooperation and coordination with local colleges and define the resources available at each institution. (4) Assess the library's own resources—the staff, materials, and services available for such a new service. (5) Prepare a written proposal outlining the program objectives, development, responsibilities, and personnel required. (6) If the proposal includes a budget, identify appropriate funding agencies and seek funding that will include adequate amounts for a paid advertising program for recruiting independent students. (7) Utilize faculty members to prepare study guides and reading lists. (8) Train librarians who will provide the direct services and faculty members who will conduct workshops, help sessions, and tutoring services. (9) Obtain resource and informational materials from all participating agencies, organizations, and institutions (such as accrediting associations, testing services, and area colleges) to be distributed as part of the service. (10) After receiving funding and prior to implementation, prepare and distribute introductory publicity to alert the community to the program; prepare publicity materials for in-library use and for mailing designed to stimulate and maintain the interest of the independent student. (11) Prepare to add materials to the library's collections as the demand is expressed through independent students' requests. (12) Prepare for ongoing evaluation and adjust the library's program to these findings.

# IV

◻▭◻▭◻▭◻▭◻▭◻▭◻▭◻▭◻

# Organizing Satellites

Frequently in higher education innovators do not need to launch a completely separate institution to implement a new idea. Even if the existing program of existing institutions cannot be modified, permission may be won for adding the new alongside the old. Some writers claim that this technique of accretion is the most common form of academic change in higher education. As an example, they cite the addition of new courses to the curriculum—not as replacements for old courses but as "electives" complementary to them; they also cite the addition of new fields of concentration, new departments, new divisions and schools, and new degree programs (Hefferlin, 1969). By adding such units, colleges and universities

75

have expanded their educational services without disrupting their existing programs.

The most recent examples of this accretion approach to change have been the satellite structures, including cluster colleges, opened at scores of institutions during the 1960s and into the 1970s; most of these satellites are interdisciplinary or "thematic" in their programs and semiautonomous in their policies and procedures.

Enough has already been written about the origins of these cluster colleges (Gaff and associates, 1970; Dressel, 1971; Suczek, 1972; MacDonald, 1973) that we include only one example, Johnston College at the University of Redlands. The other three cases illustrate other types of satellite operations: the addition of a new unit concerned with health care and the training of new health-care specialists at the Johns Hopkins Medical Institutions; the creation of a three-year degree program at the State University of New York at Geneseo; and the adoption of the federally assisted University Year for ACTION by Pepperdine University. All four depict the "end-run" technique of avoiding the opposition to innovation by creating a separate unit for it—a separate department, office, or staff—but at the same time incorporating this relatively autonomous unit within a well-established institution.

In earlier chapters, we have emphasized the importance of determined leadership, financial support, and the stamp of legitimacy, whether from government, foundations, or well-established academic institutions. Without leadership, financial support, and such endorsement, innovations in higher education cannot succeed. The new satellite operations described in this chapter do not contradict that previous evidence. Instead, they supplement it with an additional prerequisite: some minimal toleration of the unit by present members of the institution plus some amount of autonomy or independence for the unit from existing institutional requirements. In other words, the forces, both positive and negative, which bear on the innovation from within the institution need to be taken into account.

For example, during the exploration stage, the faculty and staff of Johns Hopkins were only lukewarm toward the proposed Center for Allied Health Careers, the Office of Health Care Programs, and the provision of health care to the community. They were willing to tolerate the implementation of these ideas by their "young Turk" associates, however, because of the clear and present community support for the ideas. Similarly, administrators at SUNY at Geneseo had to persuade members of the faculty not to impede the innovation, since the faculty did not want Geneseo to become primarily an upper-division institution for community college graduates. Throughout its developmental stages Johnston College at the University of Redlands experienced tension between the ideal of extensive autonomy and the realities of institutional tradition. And, as Ann Ventre points out regarding Pepperdine's acceptance of the University Year for ACTION, Pepperdine's departments were unwilling to permit students to complete more than twelve units of work in any one field—a factor which may prolong its trial stage. Such a possibility may not be viewed with concern at Pepperdine in the light of Ventre's statement that the time element is less important than support from the administration, key faculty members, and the community, as well as the selection of a good director. In that view, the combination of forces last cited overbalances the need to be concerned about time. Such a conclusion provokes the question: How can innovators judge when one force or combination of forces bearing on an innovation at a given state of its development is more or less crucial than others? The interactive forces theory presented in Chapter Eight helps to answer that question.

To assure toleration for the new programs, the initiative of positive, personal forces within the institution (the young Turks at Johns Hopkins, administrators at Geneseo, the chancellor at Redlands, and selected students and faculty members at Pepperdine)' was required. Outside support (such as the leadership of the East Baltimore Community Corporation, the founders of Columbia at Johns Hopkins, and the founding grant for Johnston College) was, of course, helpful. But the role of these internal advocates was to win permission from their colleagues for the new venture and some leeway for its inauguration.

Innovators who start afresh by creating a separate institution, instead of attaching their innovation to an established institution, avoid this need to convince other members of the institution to accept their idea. If they succeed in creating an independent institution, they can choose colleagues already committed to the idea. But the risk of success by starting afresh rather than affiliating with an existing institution tends to outweigh this problem of affiliation. If permission can be gained to try the idea even temporarily at a well-established college or university, affiliation has many advantages—chief among them being the legitimacy gained for the idea by its very acceptance within the institution.

Thus, as long as an innovator can sense any likelihood of success at convincing the members of an existing college or university to adopt an innovation, he should take this course and abandon it only when no likelihood remains of its acceptance. Following the advice of Machiavelli, the innovator should first see whether the present structure can, with minimal modification, accomplish his plan as well as or better than any new institution. If so, attaching it as a satellite operation—parallel to rather than a replacement for the existing program—is likely to assure the greatest chance of success.

## COMMUNITY HEALTH-CARE EDUCATION: JOHNS HOPKINS MEDICAL INSTITUTIONS

MOSES S. KOCH, *president, Monroe Community College; formerly deputy director, Health Associate Programs, Johns Hopkins Medical Institutions*
ARCHIE S. GOLDEN, *director, Health Associate Programs, Johns Hopkins Medical Institutions*

The Johns Hopkins Medical Institutions in Baltimore, one of the most prestigious centers of medical learning in the world, did not until recently consider health-care services to the general public a major priority. Changes began to occur, however, when Hopkins, like many other inner-city institutions, could no longer afford to remain impervious to the social changes taking place during the 1960s—changes that led this institution to a community involvement previously considered outside its mission.

### Time Frame

The first new impetus occurred in 1963–64, when Johns Hopkins was asked by the developer to initiate a plan for the delivery of health care in the new city of Columbia, Maryland, a pre-planned city growing up between Baltimore and Washington, with a population projection of approximately 110,000 by 1980. Eventually, after considerable discussion and despite some internal inertia, in October 1969 a clinic was started, for all people who enrolled in a prepayment group medical plan. Concurrently, Johns Hopkins became involved with the East Baltimore community (where the hospital, the School of Medicine, and the School of Hygiene and Public Health are located) in the planning and development of a comprehensive health-care-delivery program in the inner city. Again after much debate, in the spring of 1968 the East Baltimore Community Corporation was formed to develop a community-run health program. Its board consists of seventeen inner-city residents and two Johns Hopkins physicians. The corporation has organized the East Baltimore Medical Plan in collaboration with Hopkins for the delivery of comprehensive health care to disadvantaged residents of the surrounding area.

The Hopkins Medical Institutions responded to these newly recognized community responsibilities by a change in their own administrative structure. An Office of Health Care Programs responsible to three medical institutions and the university was established in 1968, to encourage collective involvement and commitment. In articulation with the East Baltimore Community Corporation, an innovative staffing pattern for the new medical plan was developed. This pattern of health-care delivery called for two new levels of nonphysician health-care personnel, termed Family Health Advocate and Family Health Supervisor. This innovation necessitated the development of a new training program. Thus, in November 1970, the Office of Health Care Programs joined the East Baltimore Community Corporation in developing a program to train Family Health Advocates and Family Health Supervisors. This was a major step in a new direction for Johns Hopkins.

Initially, five nurses and a former medical corpsman were trained as Family Health Supervisors to deliver primary health care to family groups much as general practitioners have done in the past and are still doing. The Family Health Supervisor is responsible for making diagnosis and treatment plans for most of the mild to moderate health problems. He performs health maintenance on

individuals and families and recognizes problems which need re-
ferral to a physician or other health specialist.

Twelve community residents were trained as Family Health
Advocates; some of them were not high school graduates. The
Family Health Advocate is prepared to function as the "front-line
worker" in first contact with the community in the clinic or in the
home. In addition to taking most of the history, the advocate also
can do a number of tasks in physical examination and laboratory
testing. The advocate can gain intimate knowledge of home life by
visiting and is able to lead in formulating and implementing many
aspects of the treatment plan because he knows most completely the
resources available to the patient and his family.

In November 1971, the East Baltimore Health Center
opened, and newly developed family-health teams began delivering
health care there as planned. The East Baltimore Health Center
provides comprehensive health care for five thousand neighborhood
residents; hospital or specialty care is provided by the Johns Hopkins Medical Institutions.

## Critical Decision Points

The first critical decision point was whether an institution,
such as Johns Hopkins, should make a commitment to community
work. Many faculty members maintained, and still do, that the
institution should continue to do what it has been doing well for
the past decades and that social change should be left to public
institutions. Certain faculty felt that community involvement would
mean a cutback in funds for basic medical research. Others, however, held that this change must take place. The latter group has
prevailed, although not without difficulties; and, so far, it has been
demonstrated that a university can make this decision without
putting in jeopardy its other recognized commitments.

Another decision point is related to the question of control
over the health-care and the training programs. Although community control of health programs is not a panacea, it is certainly
an important element in the attempt to bring quality health services
to all of the local residents. Yet, how does a strong, powerful health
institution aid—without controlling—an underprivileged commu-

nity in developing its health program? This question has no simple answer. If the medical institution controls the money, it definitely controls the program. If the community controls the money, it may or may not run the program, depending on who controls the board. Apparently, the Baltimore situation has evolved fairly well; the East Baltimore Community Corporation has become stronger and does manage the health program (seventeen of its nineteen board members are local community residents), and Johns Hopkins continues to work with this corporation.

Another extremely important question is whether blacks and whites can work as colleagues, especially in leadership positions. The key factor seems to be the ability of the participants to develop a mutual trust. At Hopkins, the health professionals and the community members learned a great deal about each other and the organization of community health. An important corollary of this, at least at the outset, is the importance of involving only those institutional personnel who are deeply committed to social change in health systems. In the main, the Young Turks have maintained and enlarged this movement and the commitment of the university to the community.

## Productivity

Johns Hopkins Medical School was one of the first to introduce the clinical clerkship to this country. This is a method of in-depth student work with patients in a hospital ward or an outpatient department. Although this method successfully trains students to care for very sick individuals, it is hampered by the artificial hospital environment. In the program for health advocates and associates, however, these methods are being supplemented by an emphasis on practicums in real-life situations. The health problems of persons in these situations have been used as focal points for learning specific principles, concepts, and practices in health care. Thus, a deductive method of learning has evolved. The course Family Health Studies, which embodies this concept, encompasses 180 hours of the basic 860-hour family-health team program.

For the first time, Hopkins is deliberately training together persons who are at different levels of educational attainment and from different professional groups and who are training for different levels of jobs. Not all of the training of the health advocate and the health supervisor is shared; at times, some of the advocates' training is convergent with the training of health supervisors; at other times, the groups diverge and are separate. For example, most of the seminar discussions have been shared by both groups, most of the technical instruction has been given separately, and the clinical practicums have varied between the separate grouping and the shared learning. However, the important institutional phenomenon has been the consciously designed pattern of joining education between two related occupational groups which are trained to work together, but at two different occupational levels.

### Future Course

A three-step program of health advocate, health assistant, and health associate—rather than the two levels of health advocate and health supervisor—is planned for the future. The career will have multiple entry and exit points, allowing for both vertical and horizontal mobility. This innovation has led the university to work directly with local community colleges in developing joint programs through which community colleges would grant academic credits for the clinical training provided by Hopkins. In this connection, new associate-degree curriculums, as well as new courses which emphasize the cooperative approach, are planned.

Building on its Center for Allied Health Careers, opened in 1970, Johns Hopkins is now making the center a part of a School of Health Services for the education of nurses, health associates, and medical technologists at the baccalaureate level. With approval of this action by the university's board of trustees, the university is now able to offer third-year and fourth-year programs as a continuation of those available through the community college associate-degree programs.

Finally, these new steps have brought about the adoption of the principle of equivalency and performance testing, so that persons entering such programs at any level—high school, community college, or Hopkins baccalaureate—will receive maximum recognition and academic credits for their previous and pertinent education and/or experience.

The innovative three-step family-health-career program is almost certain to remain an element of institutional form and to be incorporated in the new School of Health Services. Another almost certain outcome will be the extension of the present relations with regional community colleges in developing new curricula, particularly as these are focused on medical specialties of community need.

## Articulation

Much of the articulation among the several university components involved in the innovation has occurred as a result of the work which went into the preparation and operation of the training program. Frequent consultation was necessary with the various departments involved in the training, such as obstetrics or psychiatry. The departments became even more intimately involved when the students began their practicum work within them.

Articulation with agencies external to Hopkins also occurred with certain agencies involved in program planning and operation—such agencies as the City Health Department, the Martin Luther King Parent-Child Center, and the City Department of Social Services. The Johns Hopkins Center for Allied Health Careers has also developed various health-career training programs with high schools and community colleges. This relationship serves as a key link in articulating the program into the educational structure, with increasing possibility of transforming pertinent experience and training into academic credits.

Here, a serious question arises: Can graduate-degree-granting institutions, such as Johns Hopkins, develop programs with community colleges? Traditionally, there has been a sharp demarcation between these two types of educational agencies, with universities viewing the two-year colleges as second-class citizens. Several key factors broke down these barriers at Johns Hopkins. A former community college president was named as associate director of the Center for Allied Health Careers. This opened many doors previously closed. The director of the center made a particular point of developing good relationships with the colleges. In addition, the center demonstrated its good faith in the college-level education by developing new health curricula jointly with the community colleges, with full credit being given toward baccalaureate education. Because this center will be a component of the new School of Health Services of the university, articulation will also take place with other major professional divisions, such as the School of Medicine, the School of Hygiene and Public Health, and the Johns Hopkins Hospital.

Finally, the major articulation should be that of the training of health professionals with the service systems in which they will work. The Hopkins relationships with the health plans in Columbia, Maryland, and in East Baltimore are an exemplary setting for the preparation of health workers for the future health system represented by these programs.

## THREE-YEAR BACCALAUREATE PROGRAM: STATE UNIVERSITY OF NEW YORK AT GENESEO

CHARLES W. MEINERT, *associate in higher education, New York State Department of Education*

Many new forms of articulation between high school and college are aimed at shortening the time needed to complete the secondary school-college sequence to less than the traditional eight years. Students may be admitted to college after their junior year in high school, or they may enroll in "bridge-year" programs that combine aspects of the senior year in high school and the freshman year in college. The approach discussed here preserves the standard four years of high school but shortens the total high school–college span by reducing the baccalaureate program to three years' duration. This is a quantitative reduction in semester hours from the usual 120 to approximately 90. One of the oldest of the current experiments of this type, the three-year program at the State University of New York College at Geneseo, is not a peripheral program that operates outside the institutional mainstream but is an attempt to expand the options within the basic operation of the college. Half of the freshman class entering in fall 1972 were accepted into the new program (380 of 760). The scope of the Geneseo experiment also provides a scale which permits easier identification of the strengths and problems of this approach, and it provides more meaningful statistical data.

### Description and Analysis

*Theoretical basis.* The philosophical and educational basis for time-shortened degree programs is the belief that a large proportion of high school graduates are physically, socially, and intellectually more advanced than their parents were at that respective point in their lives. Much of what is taught in the typical college freshman year is a repetition of the high school curriculum, and much of the social development formerly associated with the freshman year in college has already occurred. These views are stated in the Carnegie Commission publication *Less Time, More Options* (1971) and are supported by the research and writings of men like E. Everard Blanchard at DePaul University and Kenneth Keniston at Yale.

Coupled with this situation has been the tendency to force students to defer adult responsibilities and careers several years because of the press for more advanced credentials to enter the work force. These pressures have alienated many students. What is needed, and is apparently possible without a diminution of quality, is a shortening of the undergraduate period that will allow young people to move more rapidly into jobs or graduate/professional schools.

*The setting for experimentation.* The State University College at Geneseo, New York, seemed an unlikely place for a major educational experiment based on the preceding viewpoints. Originally established as a normal school, it began to grant baccalaureate teaching degrees in the 1940s and became a unit of the State University of New York in 1948; it offered graduate work in the 1950s and liberal arts programs in the 1960s. In addition to the normal range of liberal arts and education programs, the college offers majors in library and information science and in speech and hearing. The faculty members are highly credentialed (65 percent Ph.D., 31 percent M.A.) and are departmentally oriented.

*Motivation for experimentation.* The faculty involved in developing the program hoped to provide a better education by eliminating curricular overlapping and allowing students to accelerate their progress. There was also a desire to find an institutional role that would prevent the college from becoming primarily a transfer institution for community college graduates; to bring students from outside the normal western New York State area; and to attract academically stronger and more motivated students.

Some administrators in the SUNY central office saw the time-shortened program as an economical way to handle increased numbers of students without committing additional resources. This was particularly critical in view of the fiscal constraints at the time. Local administrators may also have seen the opportunity to establish an innovative program that would be an asset in the competition for limited funds and students. The students indicated a desire to save money and to avoid certain subjects in typical freshman core or distribution programs. Certainly, any successful academic venture must recognize and provide for the range of motives and interests that exist concerning change on any campus.

*History of development.* The idea for the development of time-shortened degree programs took shape in the central office of the state university during the winter of 1970–71. These thoughts were stimulated by conversations with Carnegie personnel and by related publications. As a first step in translating the concept into action, administrative and faculty representatives of selected units of the university were invited by the SUNY central office and the Carnegie Corporation to a three-day meeting in June 1971. Geneseo was represented by three administrators and five full professors. The Geneseo delegation recommended starting a small experimental program in the fall of 1971 and establishment of a planning committee immediately. An experimental group of approximately one hundred would be recruited from students already admitted in the 1971 freshman class who had declared majors in biology, economics, English, history, physics, or political science.

Fourteen people, including two administrators, were appointed to the planning committee. The group was heavily weighted with full professors and department chairmen. In mid-August another meeting with central office staff of SUNY was held to prepare a proposal for Carnegie Corporation funds. Although the Geneseo committee members were not in total agreement on all twenty-three recommendations in the proposal, no member of the group opposed the final report.

Following this report, slightly more than one hundred first-year students were admitted to the program on a provisional basis pending faculty approval. This approval was given in September 1971, and a new development committee, proceeding from the report of the planning committee, submitted a report in February 1972. Basically, this report supported earlier recommendations with one major exception: Special core courses were abandoned in favor of comprehensive examinations in three academic areas which would allow all courses to be taken in the major or as electives. The Geneseo faculty accepted this report in April 1972 and extended the experimental period for an expanded program to five years, with a full evaluation at the end of the fourth year.

During this period of planning, contact was made with the regional and state accrediting offices, where approval was obtained for the experimental program. Additional good news was the announcement in the fall of 1971 that an $80,000 grant for three years had been received from the Carnegie Corporation of New York to help support the experiment. With support from the faculty, accrediting groups, and foundations, approximately 380 new students were admitted into the program in the fall of 1972.

Unquestionably, the major accomplishment described in the preceding history was the rapid planning and implementation with faculty approval of this institution-wide experiment. Many ideas of equal merit have perished without a trial via endless study commissions operating under the paralysis of perfection or have been relegated to the periphery in some small special division that will neither threaten nor affect the mainstream of institutional life.

It is difficult to estimate precisely what enabled Geneseo to overcome the usual faculty opposition to major institutional change. Certainly, clear administrative support while carefully involving the faculty at all stages was critical. Staffing all committees with full professors and department chairmen fully engaged those with influence and power. The committees were also given clear charges and specific constraints—providing a sense that "business as usual" was no longer adequate and that certain risks were necessary. At the same time, the risks did not appear too great, since the new program did not threaten job security, the existing power structure, or the dominance of the departmental major.

*Admission criteria.* A three-year bachelor's program could base admissions on ability to prove competency in the basic core, the criterion for waiving a year of course work. Geneseo decided to defer the issue of core competence to a later period, however, and established separate criteria for admission into its program. These included the requirement of a 2.5 predicted college grade point average, a Regents Scholarship Exam score of 200, or a combined SAT of 1200. After the initial trial year, a Committee to Evaluate Admissions Criteria submitted a minority and a majority report, both favoring a liberalization of admission. The minority report, however, urged that all freshman students admitted to Geneseo should be allowed to enter the three-year program, while the majority report favored the maintenance of the current criteria (as described above) with minor modifications. In December 1972, the minority report was accepted, and all freshmen entering in fall 1973 were invited to participate in the program.

The actual number of students who enrolled at Geneseo specifically because of the three-year program cannot yet be estimated. The one hundred plus students admitted the first year were recruited from students already admitted. The second class also entered by this method, for by the time the faculty endorsed the extension and expansion of the program, in April 1972, admission to the college for September 1972 was complete and in accord with the separate criteria mentioned above; the minority report had not yet been endorsed. Of the 1500 new students, 800 were freshmen, and all but 200 were eligible for the three-year program; 250 accepted the letter of invitation, and an additional 100 were recruited for the twenty-five departments now participating during the summer orientation sessions for all new freshmen. The admissions office did send a fact sheet describing the program to all New York State high schools in the summer of 1972 and launched a full-scale recruiting effort for the next entering class.

*The new curriculum.* The three-year program was readily accepted by Geneseo faculty primarily because the program carried minimal initial implications for curriculum change. The major components of most undergraduate programs are core courses, electives, and courses related to the academic major (the category closest to the hearts of most departmentalized faculty); and the new program did nothing to change the status quo in this area. In fact, the major could be strengthened, since departments could require up to twenty-four hours in related courses in other departments, or a total of sixty hours controlled by the major department. The astute recognition and willingness of the college leadership to work with these realities undoubtedly contributed to the implementation of the program.

Some people connected with the new program still hope that new courses with a more interdisciplinary focus will emerge; but there is no evidence at this writing to suggest or predict any substantial change in the curriculum associated with the academic major. The curricular changes that have occurred have been confined to the abolition of the core area. The only core requirement that remains is the three credits of physical education (formerly four credits). Students must demonstrate core competence by passing three area tests before the end of the third year, or they must revert to the four-year track.

*Assessment.* Three-year students have been compared with control groups of four-year students. The comparison examines four-year students of two groups: those who also declared majors in the six initial departments (noted above) as freshmen in 1971 and those who were eligible but did not enter the program in fall 1972. Evidence thus far tends to indicate that three-year students achieve a higher grade-point average than do their first year counterparts in the four-year sequence; the attrition rate is also lower for students in the experimental program.

*Financial implications.* From the perspective of the student and his parents, it is possible to reduce the cost of a baccalaureate education substantially. Under the SUNY system of differentiation by level, the three-year student pays the lower-division tuition rate for two years and the higher upper-division rate for only one year. This situation works against keeping a 120-credit graduation requirement and simply awarding thirty credits for demonstrating core competence, as a college without a differential tuition rate might do. From the standpoint of the institution, there are additional costs associated with a three-year program, particularly in its developmental period, because of additional staffing for administration, research, and academic advising. Many of these expenses are currently being underwritten by the Carnegie grant, but when it has been expended and better data are available concerning the costs of the new program, any additional expenses will most likely be passed on to students in the form of a special tuition rate or admissions fee.

From the perspective of a public university system or state legislature, the potential savings attached to the widespread use of such programs appear substantial. The same facilities and staff can accommodate many more students in a span of years, thus saving the expansion costs associated with new or enlarged public institutions. Private colleges may be attracted to such experiments, so that they can at least match the opportunities available at public institutions. Some people might prefer a degree from certain private institutions if it could be obtained in three years at a cost comparable to the cost of four years at a public institution, but from a financial viewpoint most private colleges might do better to consider an early admissions program.

*Relation to other institutions.* The articulation of the Geneseo three-year program with graduate schools, other baccalaureate institutions, and community colleges is an important issue in an era characterized by the transferring student and the press for graduate study.

The biology and political science departments investigated the attitude of graduate departments toward admission of graduates of a time-shortened degree program. In general, the criteria for admission to graduate studies include the completion of certain undergraduate courses, a solid grade-point average, and success on the Graduate Record Examination—all bases which would not penalize a three-year bachelor's student. Geneseo will not accept any transfer students, including graduates of the community or junior college, into the three-year program, since these students presumably have already completed basic liberal arts work. The implications of this policy are extremely serious for students attending a community college and clearly concern community college administrators, as evidenced by the heavy turnout of two-year college presidents and deans at a recent Teachers College (Columbia University) special seminar session devoted to the topic. In order to solve the problems caused by such a policy, community colleges could graduate associate-degree students after only one year; or they could give two years of instruction in the nonliberal core areas, and the student could then complete the bachelor's degree at a senior college in one year; or community colleges could themselves offer time-shortened bachelor's degrees.

## Establishing an Experimental Program

There are three related but distinct aspects in the process of establishing a program: making the decision to experiment, developing the experiment, and assessing the experiment. Because the close and continued involvement of faculty is basic to the success of this kind of innovation, extensive use of committees in the completion of these three aspects in the process is highly desirable. An administrative decision in favor of the project is essential, but a decision committee, comprised mainly of the most influential faculty, is also desirable and should be appointed with a clear charge and report deadline. It should focus on the potential benefits of the project and its general design. Approval should be given for a specific period of time, with limits set for the initial participation of the disciplines, faculty members, and students to be involved. An overall steering committee assigned to an administrative office is necessary to provide general supervision of the entire procedure. Continuing development should use an implementation committee with some representation from the initial decision committee to get the project underway and to revise it on the basis of further study. Assessment needs equal and separate attention, possibly involving a committee, but a full- or part-time director of assessment not emotionally committed to the program is essential. The assessment should be of a formative, not a summative, type. Early agreement on the criteria for judgment is important.

NEW METHODS FOR MEETING TRADITIONAL GOALS:
JOHNSTON COLLEGE, UNIVERSITY OF REDLANDS

EDWARD K. WILLIAMS, *director, University Without Walls Program, Johnston College*
EUGENE G. OUELLETTE, *chancellor, Johnston College*

The establishment of Johnston College in Redlands, California, was innovative in that it created a new satellite college that rejected traditional methodology while embracing traditional goals. Grading systems, departmental structure, fixed curricula, credit-hour currency, conventional graduation requirements, and typical classroom procedures all were suspect. The old objectives of self-knowledge, understanding of society and one's roles in it, and pursuit of truth through the great academic disciplines were sharply reaffirmed. The challenge to the project was to find more effective ways of reaching and unifying those holistic goals.

To meet the challenge, the college set out to develop a coherent educational design that would combine innovations found separately on other campuses but never before formulated into a gestalt for academic reform at a single college. Included were learning contracts for graduation as well as for completion of separate courses; fully representational governance of the college community involving students, faculty, and administrators; extension into and use of the local civic community as a part of the instructional base; interpersonal and intergroup sensitivity training for all members of the college community, including faculty, students, and others; living-learning experiences in activities and events; and developmental concepts of student growth in which "dimensions" of time —past, present, future—and of environment—local, national, international—are accentuated. The dimensions concept provides a series of integrated interdisciplinary bases around which student programs may be organized. In this sense they are a substitute for the usual departmental structure.

Innovators at Johnston College passionately deny that their effort has been a patchwork, tinkering process. Instead, they see it as purposeful, unified change for meeting specific objectives—a mosaic with many small parts within a large comprehensible picture.

Early in the development of the program, these innovators decided that academic standards should not be compromised, that the institution should assist in the social orientation of students, and that personal growth should be supported by the institution.

Nonthreatening relationships with faculty members, sensitivity training, and varied learning opportunities, such as the University Without Walls, community training, internships, and independent study are provided. Some historically negative characteristics and practices, such as autocratic formalism in the classroom, a presumptive and punitive grading system, a numerical and nondescriptive credit-hour currency, and even political pressures within and between departments have been viewed as expendable at Johnston College.

In the graduation contract system, each student develops a long-range plan of study in consultation with individual faculty members. A contract is then negotiated with a student-faculty committee, to be updated from time to time. When the terms of the contract have been completed, another committee verifies that fact, endorses a précis of the student's college career, and recommends graduation to the faculty and the board.

Students assume a central role in the management of Johnston's total educational program as well as their own programs. For example, the instructor shares responsibility for selection of materials with one subcommittee of students from his class, handles evaluation with another subcommittee, works out the discussion schedule with another, and so on.

Social change–oriented programs are often either too violent, too ineffectual, or both. The creation of internships as a standard method of instruction at Johnston was intended to avoid such extremes and link academic with vocational learning. Formal contracts for graduation and individual courses protect both the student and the college. The specification of what students are expected to accomplish protects them and reduces irresponsibility and capriciousness in what could otherwise be a commonplace permissive program. This result clearly contributes to the goal of the college to preserve academic integrity while developing instructional flexibility. A responsible, continuous, and open process for evaluation is needed in such a student-oriented, open instructional mode. To meet this need, the précis of a student's career has been developed as a substitute for the conventional college transcript. This evaluation procedure requires considerable work to maintain; but it has remained a central and unifying part of the system.

## Time Frame

Lead time for getting the college into operation was unusually short, amounting to only a year before classes actually began. This factor was no great disadvantage, however, given the prior decision to bring students, faculty, and staff together as a working community to design the whole academic structure. In fact, there is some indication that more lead time might merely have prolonged debate on the advisability and, later, the feasibility of the innovations, possibly even foreclosing action on them entirely.

Key points in the timing of Johnston College's development are: 1965, University of Redlands board of trustees authorizes creation of a new cluster college; 1967–1968, major funding support is given by James Graham Johnston; 1968, first chancellor is chosen, who with two faculty members and a secretarial staff constitute the planning task force; 1968–1969, board of overseers is established with academic autonomy; September 1969, all-college ten-day retreat is held; October 1969, college community is formed, governance plan is established, classes get underway; May 1970, trustees' evaluation committee is appointed; May 1971, acting chancellor is designated chancellor; October 1971, governance committee plan is accepted; January 1972, college sponsors National Symposium for Experimental Colleges; 1972–1973, evaluation by Wright Institute is completed; May 1973, first four-year class graduates; May 1973, Johnston College is independently accredited by the Western Association of Secondary Schools and Colleges.

## Key Decisions

The agreement to enlarge the University of Redlands through the creation of a new college generated a new source of competition and conflict, rival academic policies, and potential threats to the academic establishment. Decisions which followed the agreement (1) granted academic but not social autonomy to a new institution through an independent board of overseers, (2) selected a chancellor and chairman of the board who were committed to experimentation, and (3) set up a time frame that could not have been met by conventional academic planning.

Winston Churchill's contention that "we shape our buildings and then they shape us" was both illustrated and refuted by decisions made about buildings and grounds. One corner of the University of Redlands campus was allocated to Johnston College; the administration was to be housed in the lowest floor of a new library under construction. But the decision to build two dormitories and a commons building near the library in an architectural style consistent with it gave the new college needed identity. While these expensive structures imposed some economic restrictions on the college, they also helped to bring about planning for a learning community, and at the same time they established a permanent link between the parent and the new institution.

One critical academic decision, eloquently propounded by the first chairman of the board of overseers, was to establish a unified program, based on commitment to personal development, maintenance of high academic standards, and responsiveness to the needs of society. In 1969, in his now-famous "tin-lizzie" letter to the Johnston faculty members, he challenged the college to design a whole new vehicle in education, as radically new and functional as the first Model T Ford had been in its day.

A key feature of the academic component of that new vehicle at Johnston is termed *confluent education*. This concept emphasizes the pursuit of self-knowledge through interaction with others. Among the methods used are encounter groups, group therapy sessions, gestalt workshops, and sensitivity training. Students, faculty, and staff can all participate in this interpersonal training. The first enthusiasm for such training has waned at Johnston, though there is still considerable activity in this field. Some energy has been redirected toward advisor-advisee relations. The role of advisors has expanded, since advisors now help to plan graduation contracts. Advisors are also needed to plan for and evaluate wider use of off-campus experiences and the resources of other institutions. In dealing with other institutions, their chief problem has been to establish an equitable financial policy to support the students who temporarily move to Johnston. From the beginning, activities oriented toward the professions and society have flourished in the form of internships and community insight programs.

The first important governance decision was to grant the Johnston community as a whole full decision-making authority, subject only to the chancellor's veto. This decision resulted in chaos, and it caused jurisdictional conflict over the scope of Johnston's power because, although the college is relatively autonomous and separately accredited, it is nevertheless a satellite institution within the control and policy framework of the University of Redlands. For example, the university administers the library, business office, admissions, registration, alumni, and development, while the college, through its separate board of overseers, has autonomy in the areas of faculty, academic policy, curriculum, grades, and graduation requirements.

After a year and a half of tempestuous struggle, in January, 1971, the University of Redlands decided to replace the first Johnston chancellor. One of the last actions of the community in the 1970–1971 school year, pushed through by a student bloc, was to overwhelmingly defeat an alternate governance plan proposed by the university. Thus, during the second year of the college, governance was in a state of limbo and chaos, in which coherent but unsatisfactory alternatives were rejected. In late fall of 1971, however, under a new chancellor, a new committee-based governance plan was easily adopted. The new chancellor has encouraged decentralization of power while at the same time personally accepting accountability.

## Productivity

Evidence accumulated from Johnston's longitudinal studies, including personality tests, ACE data, and aptitude tests, and from other evaluators, such as the Wright Institute and various graduate and professional schools, shows the effectiveness of the college's comprehensive approach to academic improvement. Its students exceed expectations based on their aptitude scores and on their time in college. An additional indication of the college's success is its regional accreditation on its own merits, independent of the parent University of Redlands.

Other evidence of Johnston College's productivity is that it has changed the parent University of Redlands. Contracts and written evaluations are often used there now as substitutes for standard course descriptions and grades. There has been excellent cooperation in cross-enrollment and good support of off-campus programs. The university has gone beyond merely good-humored support to take seriously a few of the ideas and programs of the junior institution.

## Next Steps

The college is making a serious effort to institutionalize change—generously acknowledged in the accreditation report of the Western Association of Secondary Schools and Colleges. Johnston is challenging the prediction that a new institution, after taking some radical steps, will settle back into middle-aged conservatism and imitate itself for the next half century. Johnston has tried to ensure that next steps *will* be taken. The most obvious insurance is a committee system of governance in which students have equal or dominant power on most matters and a rotating vice-chancellorship in which three persons, respectively, simultaneously create new responses to demonstrated needs, eliminate outworn or useless programs, and preserve continuity. The plan prolongs institutional flexibility and improves internal communication. To simplify external relationships, only one of the three at any one time is designated officially as vice chancellor.

## Articulation

Johnston's plan for articulation avoids retreating from any segment of the academic world. The college has related to the world of the free university informally, through visitation and exchange, and officially, through its national symposiums. It has correlated its data gathering with the American Council on Education's study of freshman characteristics and with standardized measuring instruments. It is working with nationally planned experimentation through the Union of Experimenting Colleges and Universities. It has gone through the regional accreditation process. Johnston has helped build up a national network of cooperating institutions that will exchange students on a short-term visiting basis, and it has actively worked on facilitating the transfer of Johnston students to graduate and other schools.

## How to Plan a Similar Experiment

The Johnston experience illustrates the need for comprehensive, coordinated efforts to achieve innovations. To this end, we make these suggestions: (1) establish the size of the experiment and demand a total commitment from the people involved; (2) establish the limits of autonomy for the satellite institution; (3) establish a time frame and guarantee continuity within that specified period; (4) establish financial support with the expectation that the new experiment will not reach a break-even point during the protected period; (5) in addition to such positive guarantees, state all limits to the program in advance; (6) establish the basis for evaluation, stressing results more than form.

# UNIVERSITY YEAR FOR ACTION: PEPPERDINE UNIVERSITY

ANN VENTRE, former director, ACTION program, Pepperdine University

The University Year for ACTION is an educational program funded by the federal government and administered by the ACTION agency.* The idea was first proposed to universities in July 1971, and the first programs began in September 1971. Like all of the ACTION programs, it provides an avenue for people who

---

* ACTION administers Peace Corps, VISTA, Foster Grandparents, SCORE, ACE, and RSVP.

wish to volunteer their services to help others. The University Year for ACTION (UYA) program is unique in that students do not interrupt their academic career to volunteer. They receive university credit for the community-service work that they do. At the time of this writing, at least forty-four programs exist.

**Basic Elements**

*Work placements.* The placement has more impact on the student's overall experience than any other part of the program. During the first phase of the Pepperdine University (Los Angeles) program, no attempt was made to concentrate placements. As a result, there were twenty-seven students in sixteen different agencies. Since then, ACTION has developed a system—called Planned Impact Programming—designed to sharpen the focus of the program by limiting the number of problem areas to be attacked by the students. In this approach, at least six volunteers work together on one project; their activities may be different, but they share a common goal.

Appropriate jobs for UYA volunteers should have the following characteristics: they should be meaningful to the student and relevant to the needs of the target community and agency; they should expose the students to the social, cultural, and economic aspects of the community; they should encourage application of university coursework; and they should create opportunities for leadership and individual initiative for the student. In addition, adequate supervision should be provided for the student volunteer, and the student's progress should be determined on some regular basis. Some examples of situations which fit the above description include providing extra manpower necessary to begin a new program or a new phase of a program; helping an agency during a period of change; helping an agency experiment with a project when it could not afford to make staff commitments for such an experimental program.

*Student selection.* Students enter the program upon the approval of their university and the ACTION office. The students in the UYA program must meet federal qualifications as stipulated by ACTION. That is, the students must be at least eighteen years old (unless given special permission to participate), without serious physical or mental problems, and they must have demonstrated an interest in community service. Moreover, they must be able to work independently and to represent the college in the community. Past academic performance seems to have little bearing on either academic or job performance. The student who does best on the program is usually one who is highly motivated to help others, who is reasonably self-confident, and who is willing to work very hard.

*Academic policies.* The academic policies defined by AC-TION for UYA are minimal. A student volunteer must work one year and earn a year of university credit, and he must not be required to attend class. Each university is free to design its own requirements, courses, credit-granting procedures, and evaluation within this framework. There are as many approaches as there are universities participating in UYA; some, like Pepperdine University, adapt courses normally studied in the classroom to the unique UYA experience.

One important academic policy imposed on the UYA program by the Pepperdine University credits committee is that no student may take more than twelve units in his major or in any one field. Without this restriction, a student could complete his whole major or minor through the UYA field experience. The departments were not willing to let this happen.

The academic system works quite well, although there are some problems. Many faculty members do not have time to develop an academic program that fully utilizes the learning potential of each UYA student's job experience. Some schools have partially overcome this problem by developing core courses with regular seminars. If seminars become too frequent, the student is being forced to attend class in addition to full-time fieldwork. It seems that most attempts to increase faculty involvement also decrease the amount of freedom available to the volunteers.

*Program coordination.* The coordination of the UYA program is similar to that of many experiential learning programs. The three most difficult tasks in administering the program are negotiating successfully with the UYA national and regional staff, continuously developing new work situations for students, and maintaining a smooth relationship with the university. Many schools (including, to some extent, Pepperdine) ask the agency itself to write the initial proposal; although such a process takes a little longer, the agency's commitment to and understanding of the project is thereby enhanced.

Since UYA and ACTION are both fairly new agencies, the amount of red tape is comparatively small, but it is multiplying rapidly. As long as the UYA program at a particular university runs smoothly, demonstrates some positive results, and follows the guidelines from the regional office and the Washington office, negotiations present few problems. If a school feels that it cannot function within the guidelines defined by UYA, it should not begin the program.

Maintaining a strong, relatively positive relationship with the campus can be a major problem. In other words, when a program is new and experimental, it is carefully observed by the whole academic community, and its mistakes will be noted by everyone. One thing which has helped the UYA program at Pepperdine is the favorable and comprehensive news coverage in the campus newspaper.

### Development of the Pepperdine Program

Pepperdine University is a small, private school with about 2800 students. At the time the UYA program began, a second campus was being constructed. The old campus, where the UYA program is located, is situated in the heart of Los Angeles and was searching for new approaches to meet the demands of what had become a highly urban and largely minority population. The UYA program fit perfectly into the needs and goals of the university.

In July of 1971, the president of Pepperdine, as well as officials of other area schools, was approached with the plan for the University Year for ACTION and asked if Pepperdine were interested. He consulted with the provost of the Los Angeles campus, and both agreed that it would be an excellent program. They indicated this to ACTION and began preparations. In August 1971, a very simple proposal—outlining Pepperdine's philosophy, the university's commitment to UYA, and brief goals for the program—was written. The school hoped to begin with thirty students; a preregistration mailing brought favorable responses from approximately twenty-five. At the same time, every university staff and faculty member who knew of community projects which would fit the UYA criteria (nonprofit organizations serving the poor) was asked to compile a list of these agencies and key people in them. A small planning grant paid the expenses of the initial period. By the end of August, ACTION had verbally approved a program of thirty volunteers.

The program had strong support in the provost's office. The chairman of the communications arts department, a highly respected faculty member, went before the departmental council and the credits committee to outline the UYA program and the necessary academic procedures. The program was approved by both committees on an experimental basis.

The members of the UYA faculty committee were carefully selected by the program director and the provost. These selections were extremely important. The committee needed to represent the departments most likely to have students participating in UYA, and it needed to be composed of highly respected faculty members. It was anticipated that many of the conservative faculty would feel that UYA was not academically valid; consequently, the faculty committee members could expect to confront resistance and criticism from colleagues.

Another important—in fact, critical—decision was where to place UYA in the administrative structure of the university. If it was placed under the supervision of any one department, it would tend to serve the needs of that department alone and not be seen as open to the whole university. On the other hand, because its academic credibility needed reinforcement, it could not be placed with the urban center, which dealt mainly with nonacademic programs. When it was finally decided that the UYA program would be directly responsible to the provost, the director of the urban center objected strenuously and sought to challenge the program. The effort was not successful, but it did cause some unpleasant problems. This is an area which needs to be carefully considered in beginning any program of this nature.

If any program is to be successful, the time element is much less important than administrative support, support of key faculty members, and a receptive attitude within the community. The selection of a good director can be crucial.

## Productivity

In the first eighteen months of the University Year for AC-TION program at Pepperdine, a total of one hundred and fifteen students enrolled in UYA. Thirty-three students completed one year on the program. Twenty-six enrolled in the program but did not complete the agreed term of service; twelve of these were terminated due to unsatisfactory performance. The most common reasons for early termination other than performance were financial problems or the lack of job-related courses available to the student. In a survey by ACTION in September 1972, the supervisors rated 52 percent of student performances as excellent and 33 percent as good. No organization with which we have worked has asked to terminate the program; in fact, all have asked to continue it although that has not always been possible. Eight students have been hired by the organizations they worked for in UYA, and three were offered positions but did not accept them.

A subtle change in faculty attitudes can be attributed in part to the fact that UYA has proceeded responsibly and its students have performed well upon their return to the classroom. The faculty as a whole seems more receptive to innovation.

## Future Modification

As a result of the positive response from the students, the faculty, and the community, it is expected that the university will continue the UYA program even as federal financing is phased out. Some modifications, however, are likely. One plan being considered would offer half-time positions to students who could not devote full time to the field experience. Other modifications in the administration of the program may be necessary to reduce its cost. Since federal guidelines requiring written proposals and detailed reports will be gone, at least one staff position can be eliminated. Once federal money is withdrawn, the strict adherence to poverty-program guidelines will also disappear. The poor will remain the most frequent beneficiaries of the students' work, but the emphasis will be on community service rather than service only to the poor.

The basic concepts of the program will remain the same. It is especially important that the student offer something to the community while he is learning from the community. The student's involvement is usually greater, and the community does not feel used by the university.

# V

# Reforming Existing Institutions

To bring about academic change by reforming the operation of an existing college or university, rather than by creating a new institution or adding a satellite program to an already established one, involves relatively fewer risks for academic innovators but offers the most difficulties. The risks are fewer because the change, once it is adopted, is unlikely to be hastily abandoned. The momentum of the institution will keep it going; and, unlike the often loose ties that bind a satellite operation to its parent institution, a major reform which passes successfully through the several developmental stages of maturation is by its very nature incorporated into the day-to-day life of the entire institution. But for this same reason, such changes are the most difficult to achieve: they require that faculty, students,

**105**

and administrators give up earlier procedures and ways of behaving in order to adapt to the new. Some members of the institution may be eager to try the idea; but inevitably others will be opposed, and overcoming these negative forces requires major effort.

Bringing about change in this way is the subject of many books in the behavioral sciences and the study of organizations; and some of the strategies and tactics that can be employed are outlined in Chapter Seven. The present chapter describes seven institutions that have been able to transform their programs. They range from a well-established private liberal arts college in Colorado, which reorganized its total approach to teaching and learning through a dramatic change in its academic calendar, to community colleges in New York and California that are implementing new curricular and administrative arrangements and, finally, to an example beyond the United States—the Universidad de San Carlos in Guatemala—where a dental school is undertaking new approaches to dental training and health care and, simultaneously, to improvement of the quality of life in the local community. All of these institutions illustrate the principle that existing institutions can change. In order to do so, however, the leadership must monitor and manage the interactive forces involved to enhance the chances for the success of the innovation.

The advantages of internal reforms for the institutions involved have been obvious. At Colorado College, under its nine-block calendar and in contrast to the traditional scheduling pattern, faculty members are free to arrange their instructional time as best suited to the specific course and students; they are free to employ a variety of learning formats, including study off campus for days at a time; and the fragmentation of time among several courses on the part of both faculty and students is no longer necessary. At Westminster and William Woods Colleges, the simple fact that the two institutions were only blocks apart could not reasonably be overlooked. Students from both colleges were already interacting socially; faculty members shared similar scholarly interests; and the strengths in the sciences at one college complemented those in the humanities and fine arts at the other. Interinstitutional cooperation—even consideration of institutional merger—was not only desirable: in retrospect it appears inevitable. At the two colleges within the Coast Community College District, as part of a larger national trend, a number of faculty members were beginning to develop performance objectives for their courses and were being rewarded for this contribution through the reward system of the district. They realized, however, that no similar systematic performance objectives existed for the entire curriculum, to say nothing of system-wide objectives which would integrate the activities of administrators, faculty members, and support staff; and this realization proved to be a force which led the district to accept an invitation to participate in a project on humanistic management. And at Union College and Union County Technical Institute, both of which had been offering separate parts of a comprehensive community college program since 1959, it became obvious in the late 1960s that unless some compensatory action in relation to impending state legislation for community colleges was taken, the two institutions would turn from interinstitutional cooperation to open competition. This realization was essential to formulation of a plan to establish the innovative "clearinghouse agency" for local cooperation; enactment of the legislation sought marked the end of the stage of formulation and the start of the trial of the idea.

But even though these changes seem clearly desirable in retrospect, their advocates needed to use a variety of strategies and tactics to win approval for them. Their success stems in no small part from the techniques they employed. Even though some of the seven innovations described in this chapter have not yet passed beyond the formulation and trial stage into refinement and full institutionalization, several of these strategies and tactics employed at various stages of the change stand out:

First, most of the institutions have proceeded in a deliberate, step-by-step manner—progressing by well-scheduled partial changes through the several developmental stages to the ultimate institutionalization of the change—rather than attempting total transformation too soon. The approach that the Coast Community College District has taken to new management techniques illustrates this procedure as well as any: the change has resulted from extensive institutional planning, clearly understood stages of the project, and the use of a number of explicit "indicators" to determine the success of each phase in meeting overall objectives of the change in relation to broad institutional goals and to use in formative evaluation for subsequent improvements.

Second, as part of this deliberate process, several institutions have pretested the changes before fully implementing them. For example, Colorado College, during formulation of the modular calendar innovation, undertook an entire mock registration under its proposed calendar to discover possible problems and to change the initial plan as necessary prior to actual registration for the 1970–1971 year. Corning Community College, also during the formulation period, tested its courses in creative behavior and interpersonal relations on experimental versus control groups of entering freshmen before adopting confluent education for all students. And at Westminster and William Woods Colleges, some interinstitutional cooperation had existed as early as 1957–58, when the colleges adopted a joint policy on student conduct; and since 1968–69 several departments of the colleges, beginning with psychology, have merged their activities—giving a chance to weigh the consequences of greater institutional coordination.

Third, the institutions have avoided committing themselves inflexibly and without recourse to the change. Thus, Colorado College voted to try its unique calendar only for a two-year period before reviewing its success—and then at that time voted to extend the experiment for an additional three years for full evaluation. The setting of specific requirements of time, procedure, and evaluation is characteristic of the trial stage of an innovation and distinguishes it from the other stages of development toward institutionalization.

Colorado College also illustrates a fourth ingredient in successful change: its advocates of the new calendar took care to consider the concerns of the rest of the institution. Having struggled for years toward the goal of decreasing the teaching load, most faculty members at the college were not eager to reverse this pattern; thus, the matter of faculty load became the subject of much discussion and reassurance. In a long series of informal and formal discussions, each objection to the plan was carefully addressed and answered on the basis of academic rationales. At Westminster and William Woods, differences between the two institutions which required resolution included their disparate philosophies of education and confusion over goals, differences in their academic calendars, and faculty concern on both sides about the loss of institutional autonomy; each of these issues required resolution. In the Coast Community College District, its humanistic approach to management has been based on an in-depth exposition of the values of the members of the two colleges, in terms of the model educational community they themselves would like to have. And at Corning Community College, an unfortunate earlier experience with another curricular plan made the need to persuade reluctant faculty an especially essential tactic.

Fifth, the institutions have relied wherever possible on outside support and encouragement: the use of outside consultants at Corning and at Coast Community Colleges, of foundation funds at Colorado, of Title III funds at Westminster and William Woods, and of Guatemalan governmental officials at the Universidad de San Carlos. Even the general trend in American higher education from an emphasis on teaching to one on learning has helped Passaic County Community College base faculty reward on evidence of student success. Whether or not this force served more powerfully to promote the performance-based faculty evaluation at Passaic than the New Jersey statute on faculty tenure which permits administrative review in light of institutional goals, however, cannot be determined. As all of the forces just mentioned are reviewed collectively, their general characteristic of being not only beyond the institution but also forces that are extrapersonal—that is, not controlled by particular individuals—is striking.

Sixth, the institutions have designed their innovations to reduce the discrepancy or hiatus between the aspiration for and the achievement of high-priority institutional goals. The cooperating authors showed their recognition of the concept of hiatus by various comparable terms applied to institutional "goal" or "objective" or "mission" related to the innovation. They viewed its operation as a guide or inspiring factor at the institution rather than as an indicator of the difference between aspiration and achievement of desired end results. Thus, they described hiatus and supported the related postulates of the interactive forces theory (described in Chapter Eight), but in their own words.

Finally, these institutions illustrate a technique referred to earlier in regard to Machiavelli's fifteenth-century advice about change: they have tried as best they could to change only that which required changing, to solve the most critical problems first and allow other issues to take less precedence. Rather than stirring up alteration upon alteration, they have focused on essential tasks; and they have used the success of these changes for later adaptations. Thus, success has stimulated success, as Colorado College exemplifies. One of the points stressed by proponents of its calendar was that it would prove educationally beneficial and also would attract both donors and students—a point especially important to a private college charging relatively high tuition. On both counts this potential advantage has become a reality. Students have voted enthusiastically for retention of the plan; new foundation funds have kept arriving; and the admissions office has received up to seven applications for every available freshman space and an even higher ratio of transfer applications.

In sum, although difficult, academic change through the reform of existing institutional procedures can be successful if certain cautions are observed and skillful techniques are employed in their adoption: not only through the initiative of committed proponents and some evidence of legitimacy for the reform and not only by winning toleration for the idea—all of which are necessary for the methods of change illustrated in previous chapters. Beyond these essential elements of change management, a global conceptual framework needs to be employed; that added essential is presented as an interactive forces theory in Chapter Eight. In addition, successful educational reformers must by a variety of means help colleagues accept and adjust to the reform as they change their own activities to accommodate it. They must not merely tolerate the change as long as it only affects others; they must implement it themselves if it is to succeed. In this way, change within higher education depends on changes in the actions of individual faculty members, administrators, and students—changes which constitute a network of personal interactive forces affecting the motion of an innovation toward institutionalization. Unless changes occur in individuals whose actions are crucial to the progress of an innovation, institutional change is highly unlikely.

Among the twenty reports, fully a third point to the valuable and constructive influence of outside sources of fiscal support, such as federal grants or foundation funds. But beyond this external support, external forces were noted as critical in four of the cases— the New Jersey community college legislation for Union College and Union County Technical Institute, the New Jersey tenure law for Passaic County Community College, the community agencies in Minneapolis–St. Paul for Minnesota Metropolitan, and the federal University Year for ACTION program for Pepperdine.

It may be that narrators of innovation, such as the authors of these case studies, simply find it easier to identify and describe the influence of a few critically important individuals than that of extrapersonal social and economic forces.

## CALENDAR CHANGES: COLORADO COLLEGE

JAMES A. JOHNSON, *registrar and professor of economics, Colorado College*

A unique calendar change was introduced at Colorado College in Colorado Springs with the fall term of 1970. A century of tradition was swept aside by the elimination of the semester system with its rigid calendar and the substitution of a highly flexible, nine-block modular system. Colorado College students had typically taken four to six courses during a fifteen-week semester, with each class meeting three or four times per week for fifty minutes per class session. The faculty was settled into this same format, teaching three or four of these courses each half year. In spite of a faculty-student ratio of approximately 14 to 1, classes ranged in size from four or five in some upper-division courses to as many as 150 in a beginning course, with an all-school average of slightly more than 22 students per class.

### Structural Characteristics

The school year is divided into nine blocks (or modules) of three and one half weeks' duration. Each block is followed by a break beginning at noon on Wednesday of the fourth week and ending at 9 A.M. on the following Monday. The school year begins approximately September 1, and Block IV concludes just before Christmas. Classes resume about January 10, and Block IX ends in time to hold the annual commencement, approximately June 1.

The normal procedure is for each student to take only one course at a time during each block. A faculty member likewise normally teaches just one course at a time, and most of these last for just one block. To the extent that there is some comparability, a block course covers about the same material formerly covered in a one-semester course. Students and faculty are generally free to devote full time to the single course taken during the block.

Each class has a room reserved exclusively for its use, and faculty and students are free to set their own meeting times according to the needs of the course. Classes may meet as long and as often as is deemed necessary by the instructor and by the students. Only two restrictions are imposed by the college. Classes must convene at 9 A.M. on the first day of the block and must end not later than noon on the last day. Between the opening and closing of the block, the format is completely flexible, with no governing college rules whatsoever.

Although the usual procedure is for students and faculty to be involved in only one course at a time, there are other options available. Two blocks may be joined together to form a two-block course. This enables a department to offer approximately one year of work in a single course (such as a year of beginning language, economics, or geology). Although the student and teacher are involved in a single effort, the course runs for seven weeks rather than three and one half. At least one department (education) has linked three blocks together to accommodate its practice-teaching course. Whenever blocks are linked together, the four-and-one-half-day break between blocks must be observed. No faculty member has the option of violating this break.

A second option permits an instructor to offer two courses at a time—one in the morning and one in the afternoon—covering a ten-and-one-half-week period, or three full blocks. Students electing this option must also take two courses (although not necessarily from the same faculty member) in order to receive full credit for the three blocks. This option has not proved to be popular, and offerings in this format have declined since the new program was adopted.

The last option was included for the purpose of accommodating skill courses such as dance, practical music, physical education, and language-skill maintenance. These courses are spread over four or five blocks and carry only one fourth as much credit as a block course. The student takes these courses in addition to his regular course, and the time schedule must be flexible enough to prevent these adjunct studies from interfering with regular courses.

In spite of the available options, it should again be emphasized that the most popular course remains the one-block type. The unpopularity of longer options has caused many departments to rethink their offerings.

## Graduation Requirements

Each full-block course earns a student one unit of credit; likewise, a two-block course earns two units; and so on. Thirty-four units are required for graduation. At least three of these units must be in the social sciences, three in the humanities, and three in the natural sciences. Since there are nine blocks per year, or thirty-six over a four-year period, a student may sit out or fail up to two blocks and still graduate on time without taking any adjunct courses or attending a summer session. A college rule forbidding any student to take more than one course at a time is rigidly enforced. For transfer purposes one unit of credit is equal to three and a half semester hours or five and one fourth quarter hours of credit.

## Objectives

The proposal was debated for nearly a year in formal sessions and in informal gatherings involving faculty, students, administration, and members of the board of trustees. It had the solid backing of the administration and several influential faculty members.

Supporters believed that it would accomplish several important objectives. Foremost, of course, was the belief that greater educational values could be achieved through the implementation of the new format. The anticipated advantages were not to be considered as objectives in themselves but as contributions to the overall goal of improving the academic program at Colorado College.

Those favoring the new program hoped that it would significantly reduce class size. It was argued that increased efficiency in faculty and student time would also be achieved. Since students were taking several courses at a time and faculty were teaching at least three during each semester, their time was fragmented and they were often torn between spending time on one course at the expense of another. Examinations and papers scheduled at the same time in several courses caused the student to continually face a series of crises.

Proponents also felt that greater educational values could be achieved by permitting a variety of learning formats. It would also be possible for classes to move off campus. Archeology, biology, geology, language, and sociology classes could spend days (or weeks) in the field. Supporters also hoped that the adoption of a totally new format of higher education would make Colorado College more attractive to prospective students and potential donors.

## Initial Objections

Opponents pointed out many problems. They agreed that average class size would be reduced; they pointed out, however, that a potential bimodal distribution would benefit few faculty and possibly work hardships on others. Also something else was likely to happen at the other end of the scale. Students would be taking slightly fewer courses per year (nine as opposed to the former ten to twelve), and to the extent that students took fewer courses it was assumed that they would cut their least popular courses first; thus, small courses might be even smaller. Certainly there might be many courses that could not be taught well on a tutorial basis, although enrollment might force the professor to use that format.

Opponents also pointed out that efficiency of student and faculty time might be reduced. Perhaps time stealing is an advantage rather than a disadvantage. A student may not want to devote an equal share of his time to all of his courses. Under the traditional system the student can apportion his time as he deems necessary. Faculty members do not necessarily need to spend exactly the same amount of time preparing for each course, but this would be the only option available. Opponents also wondered at the wisdom of voting themselves a 50 percent increase in teaching load (in terms of number of courses taught) after spending many years fighting to reduce the number of courses taught per year.

Lastly, everyone agreed that physical facilities presented a serious problem. The number of course rooms needed changed from approximately 55 to about 130—one for each member of the faculty teaching in a particular block. Every possible space that might be used as a course room was surveyed prior to the passage, including large offices, dormitory lounges, fraternity and sorority lounges, and student and faculty meeting rooms. Eventually, the necessary 130 rooms were found.

### Actual Experience

Not all of the objectives have been met in the first years, and some of them may never be achieved. On the other hand, most of the problems foreseen by opponents have materialized, although they do not appear as serious as originally anticipated.

Every measure indicates that the quality of education has improved, and this alone may outweigh most of the problems which have developed. The almost unlimited flexibility offered has significantly improved the ability of some instructors to present the desired material to students.

The opportunity to move off campus for a day or a week or for one or two blocks has proved to be a great advantage to many instructors. In only a couple of cases has an off-campus experience been unprofitable. The ability to meet as often and for as long as desired has undoubtedly improved the quality of the educational experience in many courses.

Class size continues to be a problem. Popular classes do readily fill to the maximum limit of twenty-five, and less popular classes have had problems attracting enough students to make discussion meaningful. Although average class size has fallen to the actual faculty-student ratio of approximately fourteen, there is a bimodal distribution; nearly 40 percent of all classes have twenty or more enrollees, and about 35 percent have fewer than fourteen. Additional full-time faculty, shifting as vacancies occur, and the use of part-time faculty will alleviate the problem, but it will never be completely solved.

The absence of academic conflicts for students and faculty is certainly an advantage, although the inability to apportion time among several courses is, as expected, somewhat of a disadvantage. There is no real way to accurately weigh one against the other, but in the opinion of students the advantages are greater.

Most faculty members feel that they are working harder but accomplishing more. There is a concern that they lack adequate time for research and professional development as well as for leisure and extracurricular activities. Some adjustments in faculty teaching loads may be made in the future, but this would have a tendency to compound the class-size problem.

The applications for admission have significantly increased during the past three years, and there is evidence that the adoption of the modular system has played a major role in this increase. The admissions office received nearly 3100 applications during 1972–73 for the 425 available freshman spaces. Transfer applications are running at an even higher ratio.

**Evaluation**

The results of three annual surveys supervised by the assistant dean of the college have been quite consistent, with no major opinion changes noted over the time span involved.

Students clearly prefer the one-block course, and a large majority dislike the half-course option. Students and faculty feel that class attendance has significantly increased, and both feel that students are better prepared for classroom work than under the traditional system. Half of the 1973 graduates feel that they are better prepared for postgraduate plans, 18 percent feel less well prepared, and 32 percent feel that they are equally well prepared.

Eighty-nine percent of all students surveyed indicated that their reaction to the block system was moderately to highly favorable, with 76 percent of the faculty reacting similarly; 6 percent of all students surveyed and 20 percent of all faculty indicated a moderate to highly unfavorable reaction, with the highly unfavorable reactions being 1 percent and 3 percent respectively. Eighty-one percent of the students believe that the Colorado College plan should be continued as is or with minor modifications. In 1972–73 the faculty voted almost unanimously to continue the program for three years beyond the initial two-year experimental period.

## Further Innovations

Although the plan in itself was a major innovation, it is primarily a tool for enabling the college to experiment with a large number of educational programs that would otherwise be very difficult to implement. Most conventional calendars are simply not flexible enough to permit these types of innovations. Off-campus experiences are much easier under the new calendar and can be much more profitable. The German, French, and Spanish departments have programs enabling students to spend the last two blocks (seven weeks) in a foreign country and then remain through the summer on their own if they so desire.

Of equal importance is the ability to move a class off campus for a day, two days, or a week or more. Under the plan, field trips for geology, biology, economics, or any other course are easily arranged. Governmental and political participation courses are easily handled under this calendar.

The college introduced a "Western Civilization" and a "Medieval Studies" program during the 1973–74 academic year. Each of these courses is three blocks long, and students share a common experience. Faculty members participate in the program for only one block on an intensive basis, but the plan will enable them to return to the course for a day or two days in order to provide continuity to the program.

## A Guide to Implementation

To ensure a smooth implementation of a major calendar change, we suggest the following sequence of events: (1) appointment of a coordinator; (2) determination of college goals; (3) examination of the present program in light of these objectives;

(4) discussion of the modular concept if a majority of faculty, students, and administrators agree that the present system is incapable of meeting the objectives of the college; (5) initiation of discussion on the idea that a straight modular plan will be implemented with no other options (variations may emerge from the discussion); (6) a decision as to whether or not the college wants to proceed with the new plan; (7) development of a possible schedule for the following year by each department; (8) examination of the schedule to determine possible problems involving prerequisites within a department or throughout the college with suggestions for changes; and (9) a trial or mock registration for the following fall.

## CONFLUENT EDUCATION:
## CORNING COMMUNITY COLLEGE

ROBERT W. FREDERICK, JR., *president, Corning Community College*

The term *humanistic education* (or *behavioral education* or *affective education*) refers to educational approaches that deal with the "whole" student and the learning environment as a totality, rather than merely with the mind and the intellectual content of the subject matter. Several assumptions underlie humanistic education: (1) There is a theory and science of learning. (2) Learning environment can be structured and improved. (3) Teaching style is part of the learning environment. (4) Both impediments and positive forces affect the learning process. (5) Knowledge about each of these four assertions can be used to improve learning. Humanistic education, therefore, seeks to enhance learning through improvement of the total learning environment. Cognitive education, in contrast, is the more traditional, strictly discipline-oriented approach. Corning Community College has adopted an additional term—*confluent education*—in an attempt to blend the cognitive-learning domain with the affective-learning domain.

### Time Frame

During the latter part of the 1967–68 academic year, Corning Community College made a commitment to a massive educational program for a clientele which has not typically been college-going. Through this general effort, begun for aiding the "new student," it became quite apparent that improvement in the learning environment for these students could be profitable for other students. Humanistic education at Corning developed largely through the individual commitment and energy of several staff members interested in this new concept. Institutional support was provided in the form of money for workshops, consultants, course development, and travel to study other programs.

Our first effort at humanistic education was in the development of a formal course known as Achievement Motivation, a concept originating at the Harvard University Graduate School of Business Administration. It is essentially an entrepreneurial or contract approach to establishing goals. This course was used for Corning's "Spark" program, a euphemism for its educational-opportunity program for the "new student." In addition to the "Spark" students, in the summer of 1968 approximately one quarter of the freshman class deemed to have marginal academic backgrounds were enrolled in concentrated one-week sessions of Achievement Motivation. Other courses in the affective or behavioral domain have since been developed at the college and have become a regular part of the curriculum. The human-services curriculum is also largely based on humanistic-education principles.

Faculty are also applying humanistic principles in the classrooms of their regular courses, previously organized around traditional subject matter. The initial effort in this direction began in 1970, when the college decided to move the counselors, all of whom had had experience in affective education, into the classroom area and out of the cubicles, where the traditional approach had been to deal with the individual student. Counselors were assigned specific offices in the academic areas of the college with the explicit expectation that they would work not only with students but also with faculty on classroom problems. With this step Corning moved from merely involving itself with specific humanistic courses to the blending of the affective and cognitive—that is, into the *confluent* domain.

Implementation of humanistic education is illustrated by a study made by the director of instructional research. This study examined teaching effectiveness in the light of the total learning environment. From reactions of students, conclusions were reached that certain identifiable and controllable characteristics were either harmful or helpful to the learning environment. Based on the research, a volunteer group of faculty members went through a series of training sessions with the research director and one of the counselors to eliminate or minimize teaching characteristics that seemed harmful in the teaching situation.

A sample of a different outgrowth of the humanistic-education approach has to do with the college's effort at preadmissions advising and counseling. As an open-door institution, Corning Community College accepts all high school graduates from its service area without question. The role of the admissions office, therefore, is no longer one of selecting students; instead, it is one of working with the students who select Corning and giving them appropriate experiences to maximize their benefits from the offerings of the college. During the summer of 1972 an experimental group of thirty incoming freshmen went through a series of behavioral exercises and were matched against a control group of students. After admission in the fall of 1972 the experimental group was matched against the control group. The survival rate of the experimental group was significantly higher statistically than the survival rate of the matched control group.

One further implementation of the humanistic approach at Corning Community College is the role of the learning resources committee, an outgrowth of the more traditional library committee. In the late 1960s, after a few staff members had introduced the humanistic approach, the learning resources committee began to give its attention to this new educational style. Increasingly, this committee has served as the institutional resource for affective education. Committee members present a paper on innovation at monthly faculty meetings. Working with the dean of instruction, the learning resources committee also attempts to develop more sophisticated approaches to confluent education. The movement of humanistic education in the college stimulated a full-blown organizational development study of its governance and management structure. It analyzed all five key power centers of the campus: student government, faculty government, the president's cabinet, the dean of faculty's staff, and the dean of students' staff. Out of this analysis came a significant change in structure as well as in leadership style.

## Critical Decision Points

Humanistic education evolved in a gradual way at Corning. A few staff members with modest exposure to the power of humanistic education became interested in introducing it. Consistent with its general style at the college, the administration simply allowed these faculty members to use the resources of the institution to see where their ideas would lead them. The administrative strategy was to allow the concept to flourish or die by actively supporting and encouraging those who were interested but not forcing participation of those who were indifferent.

Through the use of such supportive techniques as faculty travel and workshop participation, as well as the visibility of the successful start, the movement spread on the campus. The further implementation of humanistic education at Corning Community College has become a major high-level priority and as such is generally recognized by the faculty as a valid and important educational tool.

One of the major barriers was the resistance by certain faculty at the outset. Because certain of the characteristics and jargon of humanistic education parallel some of that in sensitivity training, many faculty were immediately turned off, feeling that humanistic education was just another name for sensitivity training. It was only through slow and painful evolution on the campus that those faculty who had had previous negative experience with sensitivity training gradually became aware that humanistic education is indeed different.

Another major barrier has been funding. The evolution of new styles of course development is an expensive process. So is the support of training programs and the use of consultants to introduce the faculty to humanistic education. To the limits of the budget, however, the college uses travel money, special-projects money, and staff-development funds to aid faculty as they move increasingly in the direction of confluent education. Needless to say, grant money has also aided in the effort toward implementing humanistic education.

## Productivity

Corning is convinced that humanistic education has improved the quality of the offerings at the institution. A major indication of the success of humanistic education is the student reaction. For example, the Achievement Motivation course is one of the more popular courses at the college. Students come out of this course so enthusiastic that they often recommend it be required of all students. Notable also is the fact that student government and other student organizations are using behavioral techniques in working with their own groups and at their own meetings. Counselors are used as facilitators to improve the environment of decision making in student government meetings. The student government budget for 1973-74 incorporated funds for workshop and retreat experiences for students and faculty. Another indicator of the productivity of humanistic education is the general success of the "Spark" program mentioned earlier. Both the results of the research into teaching effectiveness and the success of the pilot experiment for improving faculty effectiveness are further evidence of the fact that humanistic education has enriched the educational offerings at Corning Community College.

## Future Developments

Humanistic education will probably become an institutional norm at Corning. Though certainly not all faculty members will use, or be forced to use, the philosophy and strategy of humanistic education to the same degree, most of them are now committed to the undergirding principles of humanistic education and are working toward greater involvement in this area.

A major future experiment will be the use of affective strategies to deal with critical interpersonal-relationship issues on the campus. Such issues include equal-opportunity programs and affirmative action. Strategy to deal with racial issues on the campus is taking two forms: one, the legalistic form, such as the establishment of an Equal Opportunity Office; the other, based on the affective domain, such as the appointment of a minority action director. Our assertion is that affective education ought to be useful in dealing with racially oriented behavior and the resulting tensions. We expect to raise the level of racial and minority consciousness on the campus so that whites in particular will become increasingly aware of their behavior and the ways in which they can unintentionally create a hostile environment for blacks.

### Guidelines

On the basis of our experience at Corning, we suggest the following guidelines for planning for experimentation: (1) Hire the most talented, creative, and self-generating people you can possibly afford. (2) Create a system of delegated responsibility so that the staff need not check with the president on everything they plan to do or spend (post- rather than pre-audit actions and expenditures). (3) Budget "seed" money for travel, special projects, research, and staff development (including flexibility in counting teaching load). (4) Hold out a clear educational philosophy and mission for the college. (5) Stand back and let them act.

## CROSS-REGISTRATION:
## WESTMINSTER COLLEGE AND WILLIAM WOODS COLLEGE

GALE FULLER, *director, Special Education Programs, Westminster College*

Westminster College and William Woods College, two colleges located in Fulton, Missouri, were involved by the 1960s in a cooperative program whose purpose was to increase the breadth of educational experiences available to their students without substantially increasing costs. Historically the colleges had set different goals for themselves and catered to different student populations. Each had developed disciplines where it was particularly strong and in which it could enroll more students without adding faculty or physical plant. Westminster College for men, founded in 1851, had developed strong preprofessional programs, especially in the sciences. William Woods College, established in 1870 as an academy for women, had developed strong programs in the fine arts.

Although the two institutions had coexisted in the same town since William Woods moved to Fulton, Missouri, in 1890, there had been little or no interaction between the faculties or administrators, although students socialized. Exactly what triggered the events which culminated in the development of the cooperative program is unknown. Times were good, enrollments were growing, money was no serious problem, and students were doing silly things like cramming as many live bodies as possible into telephone booths, racing wheeled beds about the countryside, pounding pianos to pieces, and engaging in panty raids.

Perhaps these two colleges were forced to acknowledge the existence of each other as a result of panty raids. Such recognition was made evident in a "Joint Administrative Statement to William Woods and Westminster Students, 1957–58." This document, hammered out by joint administrative effort during the summer of 1957, outlined the dos and don'ts of acceptable social interaction between the student bodies. Perhaps it was this act that gave birth to the spirit of cooperation and brought into focus the need for change. Following close upon this action, two other factors or elements surfaced which were influential in the development of the cooperative program: (1) a sizable minority of the Westminster faculty wanted the college to become coeducational; (2) William Woods was exploring the possibilities of becoming a four-year college. Proponents of these moves stressed the favorable conditions they saw. William Woods could furnish girls for the classes of those who desired a coed mix in their classes at Westminster, and Westminster could furnish upper-level courses for girls who were preparing to take the bachelor's degree program at William Woods. The two colleges, located only a few blocks apart, were in a position to complement each other by permitting students from each college to enroll for certain courses at the other college. Accordingly, the immediate goal of the cooperative program was the exchange of a limited number of students between the colleges to add breadth to their educational programs. (Although this cooperation developed far beyond the original purpose, we will discuss only the cross-registration of students.)

The prospect of a student-exchange program was not universally endorsed or welcomed by all potential participants, and various arguments were advanced in opposition to it. The basis of opposition was rooted not in direct competition between the colleges but in biases and prejudices held by some individuals and groups on each campus and directed toward individuals or groups on the other campus. There were those who viewed the stated goals of the colleges as sufficiently different to warrant continued segregation of the students in the classroom. Concerns of many kinds surfaced: faculty-student ratios, the disparate percentages of Ph.D.s on the two faculties, the danger of "watering down" the curriculum, the possibility of verbal and psychological pressure or abuse which might be directed toward women students in an otherwise all-male institution, suspected differences in the quality of students in the two colleges, fear that the presence of men or women in the classroom would change the entire atmosphere and dampen open and free discussion. Some pointed to the fact that the students enrolled in each college had picked their college partly because it was segregated by sex. These and other concerns and fears had to be aired and put to rest by the majority of each faculty before significant progress could be made in developing the cooperative program. The issues were tested and resolved through experimentation and implementation of the program on a very gradual and tentative basis.

## Implementation

Beginning in 1960, formal arrangements were made for a few students from William Woods College to enroll in courses at Westminster. Selection was made on the basis of each student's academic needs. It was not until 1962, after William Woods had been accredited as a four-year college, that Westminster students started attending classes on that campus. The exchange of students led to a concerted effort to explore other aspects of institutional operations where cooperation would be mutually beneficial.

The cooperative program developed to its present form over

a period of about ten years. It is only in retrospect that the changes which have been wrought can be placed on a time schedule. The colleges were sensitive to student needs and, in keeping with institutional traditions, were willing to modify college programs to facilitate student growth. Historically students were not permitted to take courses at the "other" college, and exceptions required faculty approval.

As the real problems began to emerge, they had little or nothing to do with the fears and biases expressed earlier. In practice the points of difficulty centered about college calendars, credit policies, transportation between the campuses, daily class schedules, examination schedules, registration periods, and like matters. These differences severely limited the opportunities for student exchange or cross-registration. Within an already difficult situation further restrictions were inadvertently imposed by the tradition of required courses on each campus. It was obvious from the beginning that the two colleges would have to operate on the same hourly schedule and if possible the same calendar.

In 1961–62 William Woods College adopted the six-day-a-week schedule of classes. Westminster College moved to the five-day week with the 1964–65 year, and William Woods returned to the five-day schedule the following year. These changes, made for valid but different reasons for each institution, were a source of mutual irritation. Had communication between the institutions been better, the transition to a uniform schedule could have been achieved more easily.

William Woods published the course offerings of both colleges in its registration materials for the spring 1966 semester. For the fall 1966 semester the colleges jointly published a schedule of classes to be used on both campuses. The publication of a single class schedule has been the practice since that time.

The step-by-step procedure for registering in courses on the opposite campus has also changed markedly. Initially it was necessary for students to secure permission from the academic dean of their college to take a course at the other college. By 1965, a set of detailed instructions for cross-registration was available to students at both colleges.

Beginning with the spring 1973 semester, registration was

held jointly in one location for all students. This procedure made it possible for students to consult with faculty members of either college, eliminated the need to stand in line to receive approval to enroll in a course by telephone (as was the case previously), and made it much simpler to help students revise their schedules when necessary.

Starting with the 1968–69 year the psychology departments of the two colleges merged to become one department. Subsequently some other departments followed suit and became unified departments with a single chairperson administering the department's business for both colleges. In these departments all faculty members remained fiscally and officially members of the faculty of the college with which they were affiliated at the time of merger.

This information is relevant to cross-registration in that students taking courses in a joint department need no special permission to do so. In departments which have not merged, it is still necessary for students to secure permission from the department chairman at their home institution to enroll for a course in the counterpart department at the other college.

Some courses offered on each campus still require permission from the dean or registrar of the student's home college before enrollment may be accomplished. These are, for the most part, classes which do not fall clearly into any particular department at the other college, and therefore do not have a department chairperson to approve them for the students.

## Related Fiscal Developments

As the process of joint registration was developing, the fiscal accounting of student exchange also underwent several changes. Originally exchange-student hours were computed and recorded by each college; the difference was adjusted annually and paid for at a predetermined rate. This procedure was instituted in 1962, when William Woods College was first accredited as a four-year liberal arts college. With two or three years' experience it was determined that this procedure of accounting cost more than it was worth. During the 1968–69 year the colleges agreed that it was no longer necessary to pay for differences in the number of exchange-student hours or even to keep track of them. This has been the official policy regarding fiscal accounting, although it is still necessary to keep records for grading and other academic purposes.

## Productivity

If the number of students participating in the exchange program is a reliable measure, the cooperative program has been very successful. In 1961–62, five William Woods students enrolled in courses at Westminster and no Westminster students enrolled in courses at William Woods. By the end of a decade, students from the two colleges enrolled in some 1500 exchange courses, representing approximately 5000 credit hours.

Each college has been able to strengthen its already strong programs as well as to upgrade some of its average departments. Each college has been able to draw upon the complementary strengths of the other, and neither has had to contend with the problems of developing or nurturing weaker programs or to start major new progams to meet student needs and/or demands.

## Some Policy Ramifications

A cooperative program as presented here creates some problems. Each institution must be willing to forfeit some of its autonomy. Neither college is free to change its calendar or class schedule without concurrence of the other. In the joint departments, new faculty members must meet the approval of two administrations before they are employed.

Even after a decade of cooperation, occasionally one of the colleges will react negatively to something done by the other. In the beginning the cooperative program survived because of the good will of the faculties toward each other, coupled with the obvious educational advantages for the students of both colleges. More recently the cooperative program has become a policy of the two boards of trustees. The trustees are exploring possibilities of cooperation in such other areas of functioning as student recruitment, plant maintenance, and purchasing.

In 1966 a proposal was written requesting federal Title III

funds to promote the cooperative program between the two colleges. The funds provided for 1967–68 and 1968–69 enabled the colleges to hold intercollege faculty seminars to deal with problems of curriculum improvement and to consider the development and employment of a common course-numbering system, a joint library system, merged departments, and other similar possibilities. The money hastened the process of coordination and cooperation, but in retrospect was not absolutely essential to the process. Coordination had begun before funds were available, and certainly it has continued since the funds were exhausted.

### Suggestions to Others

The Westminster and William Woods experience suggests that the first step to accomplishing a cooperative program should be the assessment of what each institution has to offer the other, honestly defining its own strengths and limitations. All possible areas of cooperation, academic and nonacademic, should be explored and none dismissed lightly. It is during exploratory considerations of possible areas of cooperation that administrators (including trustees), faculty, and staff get to know each other. It is also important to consider the wishes, desires, and needs of the student body, while keeping in mind that students may reflect the attitudes of the faculty and administration. If the cooperative program is to be successful, all parties must enter such meetings with openness and good will.

Time schedules and deadlines must be flexible and subject to revision, with the realization or even expectation that not all things go as planned. A useful, or perhaps essential, element is to schedule at predetermined intervals specific times at which the interinstitutional interactions must be reviewed and evaluated. Keeping the lines of retreat open has also been helpful; that is, either institution may back away from a program of cooperation if that program does not work as anticipated. Retaining this option seems to encourage experimentation and innovation in the cooperative domain.

### Looking Ahead

The program of student exchange appears to have functionally stabilized in its present form. What the future holds for the cooperative program is, of course, unknown. It is possible that the two colleges will merge at some future time. Another possibility is that one or the other of the colleges may become coeducational. If this were to occur, the other college might withdraw from the cooperative program. The most unlikely possibility is that the two colleges would, by mutual consent, withdraw from the cooperative program and run their programs in parallel with each other as was the case before the cooperative program came into being.

## HUMANISTIC APPROACH TO EDUCATIONAL MANAGEMENT: COAST COMMUNITY COLLEGE DISTRICT

WILLIAM D. HITT, *director, Center for Improved Education, Battelle-Columbus Laboratories*
TOM GRIPP, *director of program planning and budgeting, Coast Community College District*

The Battelle Center for Improved Education (Columbus, Ohio) and the League for Innovation in the Community College are jointly developing a humanistic model of educational management for the community college. Originally, the model was pilot-tested in three league districts: Brookdale Community College (Lincroft, New Jersey), Coast Community College District (Costa Mesa, California), and Cuyahoga Community College (Cleveland, Ohio). We will here discuss only the program in the Coast Community College District.

### Underlying Propositions

The essence of the humanistic management philosophy is summarized in the following propositions.

*Proposition 1: Education should be viewed as a human enterprise.* By "human" we mean that education should deal with the nature and potentialities of individual human beings, to help these individuals achieve self-fulfillment. By "enterprise" we mean that education should be an undertaking carried out for specific purposes. Education should be viewed as an enterprise that is planned and managed for specific purposes, and then is evaluated on the basis of how well it accomplished these purposes.

*Proposition 2: Education can be a successful enterprise through the application of science-based management.* Science-based management involves the use of tools such as management by objectives, systems analysis, needs-assessment surveys, forecasting models, cost-effectiveness analysis, resource-allocation models, and management-information systems. The main features of science-based management are incorporated within the planning-programming-budgeting-evaluation (PPBE) model. Our premise here is that science-based management, in the form of PPBE, can be adapted effectively to the management of an educational system.

*Proposition 3: An educational system can be a successful human organization through the active involvement of the broad educational community.* The human being, as a subject, looks out at the world and has some influence on this world. The human being, as an object, is controlled and manipulated by the world. Our basic idea is that people within an educational system are treated as subjects to the extent that they are allowed (and encouraged) to participate in the planning and management of the educational system. This is the human dimension of educational management.

*Proposition 4: The scientific dimension of educational management can be united with the human dimension through participative management.* Participative management allows individuals to identify with particular objectives, because these are *their* objectives. These individuals are much more likely to be motivated to work toward the accomplishment of these objectives than if objectives are handed down from above. Participative management will then serve as the bond to unite the human dimension with the scientific dimension of educational management.

## Concept of Participative Management

Three prevailing models of management found in present-day education are (1) the autocratic, (2) the laissez-faire, and (3)' the management-labor. In the autocratic model, information flows "from the top down." The organizational structure is a well-defined hierarchy, with each person knowing his or her "pecking order" in the hierarchy. Individuals are told what to do and how to do it, and they comply—or else. In the laissez-faire model of management, the administrator may administer the paperwork, but he allows a high level of autonomy throughout the institution for management of the educational process. By and large, administrators have not been trained adequately in the principles and concepts of management. The management-labor model in its present form has brought forth a true polarization of administrators and faculty. Administrators have become "management," and faculty have assumed the role of "labor." It is assumed by both sides that there is a fixed amount of power in an educational system; if one side gains in power, it then follows that the other side must lose a corresponding amount of power.

In contrast to these three management designs, the community college needs one which stresses a humanistic view of educational organization. In participative management, various groups within the educational community cooperate in formulating educational objectives and in deciding on methods of accomplishing the objectives. These persons work together in deciding what they want to do and how they plan to get there. This is the essence of participative management.

Participative management is related to, but not identical with, pure democratic management. The latter calls for rule by the majority. In contrast, participative management calls for individual responsibility and accountability. The "designated leader" might be an administrator, a faculty member, or anyone else who has assumed a leadership role for a particular area of responsibility. He has the authority to make the final decision, because he must assume the responsibility for the consequences of the decision. Rensis Likert (1961, p. 51) clearly articulates this point of individual responsibility: "The group method of supervision holds the superior fully responsible for the quality of all decisions and for their implementation. He is responsible for building his subordinates into a group which makes the best decisions and carries them out well.

The superior is accountable for all decisions, for their execution, and for their results."

## Strategy for Educational Redesign

This strategy represents the application of a twelve-step planning-programming-budgeting-evaluation approach within the context of participative management.

1. *Organize and orient planning team.* Upon board approval of the redesign project, a planning team of faculty, administrators, supportive staff, students, and representatives of the general community is organized and oriented.

2. *Develop system-wide objectives.* The planning team formulates the mission statement and system-wide objectives for the educational system. A mission statement is the ultimate "why" of the educational system. The system-wide objectives are the broad statements of purpose that delineate the mission statement; they cut across all programs and activities and serve as the guide for all subsequent steps.

3. *Assess educational needs.* A need is defined here in terms of a discrepancy between what exists and what is desired. Needs are determined by comparing a description of the existing educational system with a *criterion model,* an in-depth exposition of the values of the members of the educational community; this is a model of the school system that they would *like* to have.

4. *Estimate revenues.* Estimated revenues are any funds that are likely to be available to the educational system. Sources of funds include local taxes, tuition, state support, federal support, investment earnings, and others.

5. *Establish program structure.* A *program* is defined as a set of related activities directed toward common objectives. A *program structure* is an arrangement of programs showing their interrelations and encompassing all activities in the educational system. It is useful to begin with a *descriptive* view of the existing programs (the actual) and then move toward a *prescriptive* view (the desired).

6. *Conduct program analysis.* Program analysis, probably

the most complex of the twelve steps, involves this sequence of tasks: (a) specify program objectives consistent with system-wide objectives; (b) identify indicators of effectiveness; (c) investigate alternative approaches to the accomplishment of program objectives; (d) identify program constraints; (e) evaluate the alternative approaches on the basis of estimated effectiveness and estimated cost; (f) select recommended alternatives; (g) prepare program proposals.

7. *Develop program budget.* Resource requirements are delineated in a program-budget format, which is designed in accordance with the program structure. There is a fundamental difference between the format of the traditional line-item budget and that of the program budget: the line-item approach is directed toward inputs, whereas the program-budget approach is directed toward outputs.

8. *Allocate resources.* This allocation is based upon the estimated budget requirements and the estimated revenue. Since cost requirements typically exceed available resources, Step 8 must be recycled back to Step 7 to reach a "match" between them.

9. *Prepare operational plan.* A multiyear operational plan for the educational system as a whole is then prepared, including an explicit and systematic formulation of objectives, together with a description of the procedures, resources, and schedules which will be used to achieve those objectives in the environment anticipated.

10. *Develop information system.* An information system must be designed to collect, store, and report all significant data pertaining to the plan during the period of implementation. In subsequent cycles of the planning process, the data collected in the information system can be of great value to the planning process.

11. *Implement the plan.* After approval by the board, the plan is put into operation in accordance with a specified time schedule. The responsibility for assuring that each selected alternative is implemented according to plan should be assigned to the appropriate person in the educational system. All people within the educational system who are influenced by the plan but were not actively involved in the planning process must be provided adequate orientation regarding the plan and how it affects them.

12. *Evaluate and revise.* Formative program evaluation

should take place on a continuing basis. Modifications are made in the actual operation of the programs as deemed necessary from the results of the evaluation.

This twelve-step process represents a broad strategy for educational redesign. The sequence of steps should be repeated over time because planning should be viewed as a continuous process. Also, the membership of people on the planning team can be rotated over time. This provides for wider participation of the educational community, and higher interest and enthusiasm among the participants.

## A Case Study

Combining management by objectives *and* participative management provides the basis for humanistic management in the Coast Community College District. Orange Coast College, established in 1947, and Golden West College, which opened its doors in 1966, currently enroll approximately 45,000 students in all programs. Combined staff include nearly six hundred full-time instructors and some forty administrators. Agriculture, manufacturing, and recreation are primary industries in the community. The racial distribution in the district is approximately 2 percent black, 8 percent Mexican-American, and 90 percent Caucasian; and the colleges' enrollment patterns are similar.

The use of educational objectives began in the Coast District perhaps not unlike similar beginnings in colleges across the nation. A few instructors taking graduate school courses in writing course objectives, an enterprising dean of instruction offering faculty the option of being evaluated on the basis of their course objectives, and an awakening interest by district staff in supporting such efforts were the first signs. These were followed by faculty fellowship awards to encourage the use of objectives, by training programs in the writing of instructional objectives, and by in-service contracts giving salary schedule credit for innovative teaching programs utilizing objectives. All efforts were voluntary and resulted in 70 percent of all instructors employing objectives in the courses they taught. Despite this accomplishment, a major component was missing. A major portion of the institution was organized to march forward in a systematic manner, but there was no clear agreement on the direction to take. Instructors had their objectives; but administrators, in their zeal to encourage faculty efforts, had forgotten to write theirs. Further, there were no agreed-upon system-wide objectives to relate the instructional objectives to—a somewhat common situation in community colleges. The problem was clear enough: there was no clearly defined hierarchy of objectives, moving from institutional philosophy to system-wide objectives to program objectives to institutional objectives. There were, therefore, not just instructional programs which needed organizing and systematizing *but also* support programs, *including the administrative,* which had the same need. It was this dilemma, then, that provided the impetus for the humanistic and participative program of management by objectives described here.

*Selecting a coordinator.* The individual selected for this position should be able to motivate people and to instill in them a feeling of confidence in him and the project. All participants had to feel that the goals selected were *their* objectives, that the means for reaching the goals were designed by them, and that they, as members of the college "community," would evaluate their own success at meeting the objectives.

*Organizing the planning team.* Faculty, students, and administrators or supportive staff, as well as the community at large and the board of trustees, were represented to ensure full participation in the acceptance of the process. The necessity of training in the use of management skills did limit the team membership.

It was extremely important to announce the first meeting with a personal letter suggesting that the individual was a *key* member, absolutely essential to the success of the project. The following specific activities of the planning team were discussed: (1) assisting in administering educational-needs survey, (2) establishing institutional goals with priorities on basis of needs survey and other relevant data, (3) designing program structure, (4) helping staff members develop program objectives and evaluation criteria, (5) estimating available resources (multiple year), (6) coordinating program analysis and preparation of program budgets, (7) recommending resource allocation, (8) assessing program performances as budget is executed, and (9) preparing a public report and reviewing institutional goals and program objectives for revision.

*Assessing the needs.* Careful administration of an exhaustive needs-assessment survey greatly enhanced its successful use as a means of establishing priorities. Each member of the planning team was responsible for administering the version of the form suitable for the group he represented. Care was taken not to code survey forms or force everyone to participate. The form used, however, should not preclude the discovery of previously unknown needs.

*Designing a program structure.* The needs assessed and appropriately related goals became guidelines for examining the college's existing program structure. A program for this purpose involved a series of independent, closely related services and/or activities progressing toward or contributing to a common objective or set of allied objectives.

The program structure provided the basis for bringing together all the elements of accountability, permitting the display of objectives, of the programs designed to meet these objectives together with their costs, and of data accumulated for evaluating these programs. Subprograms or activities were analyzed or compared with others in different areas. Basic indicators were established for each objective so that the degree to which the institution was successful in attaining it could be measured. One such system-wide objective was phrased as follows: "to enable students to get their first two years of higher education at *low cost,* and *be able to transfer smoothly and successfully* to a four-year school."

Establishing program objectives, determining their priorities, and evaluating how well they were being achieved were the most significant activities toward making the Coast District accountable.

## Summing Up

The broad aim of the project described here is to help community colleges improve the effectiveness of their educational management through the use of participative management by objectives. In support of this aim are four project objectives: to develop an operational-management model, to develop a management-training system, to develop a management guide, and to disseminate the results of the total management program on a national basis.

Active participation in this management project has the potential for providing community colleges with the following benefits: (1) more effective educational programs for students, (2) more effective supportive programs, (3) a rational basis for the allocation of resources, (4) improved staff development and staff morale, (5) improved communication, and (6) a means of demonstrating educational accountability.

## INTERINSTITUTIONAL COOPERATION: UNION COLLEGE AND UNION COUNTY TECHNICAL INSTITUTE

KENNETH C. MACKAY, *executive director, Union County Coordinating Agency for Higher Education*

The Union County Coordinating Agency for Higher Education provides the means by which Union County in New Jersey makes immediate and extensive use of two existing educational institutions, Union College (in Cranford) and Union County Technical Institution (in Scotch Plains), to secure for the residents of the county the services and facilities of a community college. This undertaking in Union County is significant for two main reasons: (1) it provides an example of two ongoing institutions in consortium to do the work of a community college (one specializing in technical and career programs, the other in academic courses); (2) it provides tangible evidence of a "private" college involved in providing community college services and so designated both by statute and in practice.

### History

Union College was started as the first (and very experimental) federally financed two-year college under the Works Progress Administration in 1933. Serving the location in the absence of any community college legislation in New Jersey for many years, the college acquired strong local citizen support. It was organized as an independent two-year institution, dependent mostly upon student tuition. So Union Junior College (later Union College) was continuing in the 1960s, when community college legislation came to New Jersey.

Meanwhile, in 1959 the public Union County Technical Institute had been founded under provisions of a New Jersey law providing for high school and post–high school vocational and technical training. Inasmuch as the Union College programs had developed mainly as academic and transfer courses at the collegiate level, the appearance of the technical institute supplemented the services of the college. A lively degree of cooperation developed, and leading citizens assisted and advised both schools. The presidents of the two institutions met often and worked closely together. Both served on a special committee appointed to look into the needs in higher education in the county. By this time it was evident that both schools were providing many of the services of a community college.

As the proposed legislation for a state system of two-year colleges came before the legislature, assemblymen and the state senator from Union County (all of whom had been well informed of the ongoing resources the county enjoyed in having Union College and Union County Technical Institute) sponsored successfully a rider to the state community college law enabling the county to contract for two-year-college services. This was followed up with legislation in 1969 establishing the Union County Coordinating Agency for Higher Education, with its own local nine-member board. Appointments are made by the county board of freeholders. The passage of the enabling legislation and its implementation through appropriation and endorsement at the county level (in New Jersey state and county are about equally responsible for financial support of community colleges) were notably achieved through full bipartisan support. The proposal was at no time a political issue.

Perhaps one means of measuring properly the significance of this particular experiment in cooperation and the forces surrounding it is to consider the alternative. In those years when the Union

County plan was being ratified, many other New Jersey counties were embarking upon new community colleges. The capital costs alone ranged from six to twenty-five million dollars. It is estimated that for a county the size of Union the initial capital costs would have been at least ten million dollars and would have reached twenty million dollars quickly in a necessary second stage of development. Moreover, new colleges had to assemble administrators and staff and faculty, purchase equipment, build libraries, assemble programs, and do a host of other things before even opening their doors. Beyond this, they would have to wait several years to demonstrate their entitlement to regional accreditation. All this Union County had going for it right from the start.

**The Plan**

The agency, established in 1969 and functioning ever since then, coordinates the operations and facilities of the two institutions for the maximum service of the citizens of Union County; collects state and county education allocations; and, in accordance with contractual arrangements made with each institution, reimburses these institutions for services rendered. This is done in accordance with the provisions of Chapter 180, Laws of 1968 of New Jersey, a special act providing for the establishment of such an agency in a county desiring to avail itself of existing independent two-year-college facilities. In 1969, contracts were drawn up and signed between the agency and the college, between the agency and the institute, and between the college and the institute. This triangulation of agreements enables the agency to procure educational services from the two institutions and to compensate for the rendering of such services in accordance with county budgetary provisions and with the approval of the chancellor and the state board of higher education. It also enables the two institutions, through their own contract, to offer special programs by which students on one campus may take courses on the other; and it specifically provides that Union County Technical Institute students in approved college-level programs will receive the Associate in Applied Science degree bestowed by Union College by authority of the state board of higher education. These articles of agreement were approved by the chancellor and the state board of higher education in 1969 and went into immediate effect. This marked a milestone in New Jersey education for the utilization of resources, both independent and public, cooperating together to widen educational opportunity and avoiding costly and inefficient duplication of programs and facilities. The relationship is not managerial. It is supervisory, advisory, and visitorial.

Each institution has the opportunity to shape creatively its own character and role. At the same time, through the agency the two institutions coordinate their programs and facilities as much as possible with each other for the welfare of the entire county.

Each institution has its own distinctive educational offerings. The programs at Union County Technical Institute are primarily technical and business courses, health-related courses, programs for two years or less, designed to meet the many-faceted needs of business, industry, government agencies, and the professional and semiprofessional demands of the county. Union College, developing in a tradition of close cooperation with four-year colleges and universities dating back to its founding in 1933, has emphasized curricula in the liberal arts, science, engineering, and business administration. The offerings in evening, special, and continuing education are expanding quickly on both campuses.

In accordance with the arrangement provided for by statute and in the contracts with Union College and Union County Technical Institute, the agency receives monies from the state and the county and then, in turn, forwards payments to both institutions for proportionate services rendered. The county and state assistance made possible under this arrangement immediately enabled Union College to lower its tuition for full-time students resident in Union County; this singular achievement in lowering tuition was of invaluable assistance to hundreds of Union County students and their families. When the announcement of tuition reduction was made, it attracted wide attention. Moreover, the greatly increased state assistance has made it possible for Union County Technical Institute to retain its low tuition while lessening the direct burden upon the Union County taxpayer.

The importance of the Union County innovation in higher education in providing direct and sharp lines of communication may well turn out to be one of its most influential contributions. Through regularly scheduled meetings, systematic reports, constant contact, and recurrent review, the agency and cooperating institutions together exert a systematic effort not only to respond to the needs of the county but to improve and make more effective the existing programs and offerings. A permanent liaison committee, its members representing both the college and the institute, meets regularly to exchange views and develop joint programs. The agency, moreover, by positive teamwork with the two institutions, can provide a continuing evaluation of the scope and effectiveness of the offerings at both. The agency also is responsible for keeping the freeholders and other county officials informed of important developments in the field of higher education. Through frequent distribution of reports and a newsletter, the agency provides concise and regular information to freeholders and others; and through continued investigative and exploratory techniques, the agency seeks continually to determine the desires and concerns of the residents of the county.

## What Next?

Already within the education committee of the agency and within the appropriate committees at the two institutions there is consideration of additional innovation—for example, joint faculty committees and more flexible arrangements for cross-registration and cross-class attendance and credit. At present one problem, although not critical, is that new programs are considered first by the faculty committee at one institution and then through channels to the faculty committee at the other institution. This lengthens the time needed to give faculty and institutional endorsement to worthy new programs.

One can conceive of a time when administratively the two institutions will be tied together much more closely. Now each institution has its own president and its own administrative staff. If the two institutions do in principle and procedure move toward each other, an appropriate day will arrive when the two boards of trustees, reaching themselves for closer cooperation, will select a single executive. If the arrangement should break down, however, a certain element of polarity will of course be produced, and the two institutions could conceivably go their own ways. This eventuality, which of course would be both costly and unfortunate, does not seem to be a likely prospect at all. Too much success attends the present system.

## Articulation

Articulation occurs at a number of levels: (a) the systematic reporting of the presidents of both institutions at the bimonthly meetings of the agency; (b) the regularly scheduled sessions of the liaison committee composed of representatives of both institutions for the purpose of articulation; (c) the custom of the agency in sponsoring so-called triangle luncheons and meetings at which subject-matter areas are represented; (d) the establishment recently of the new office of Dean of Educational Development. This officer reports directly to the two presidents and to the executive director of the agency, and his position is designed primarily to promote articulation among Union College, Union County Technical Institute, and the coordinating agency.

## Guidelines

Based on the Union County experience, the following steps should be observed by any analogous set of institutions desiring to serve a public purpose in making facilities and programs available in a partnership with a city or region: (1) Maintain the fullest communication with other collegiate institutions in the area and with the governing authorities. (2) Put into practice plans for cross-registration, interlibrary loan, and other aspects of college consortium. (3) Marshal facts and figures to show that this plan can increase productivity for the area and can avoid costly duplication and construction costs. (4) Make certain that legal and statutory requirements are fulfilled and that, if necessary, proper enabling legislation is enacted. (5) Be neither defensive nor defeatist in proposing the arrangement. That the plan should be established "to pull a college out of financial trouble" is the worst of justifications. If a private college is unable to maintain its plan because of declining enrollment, an excellent alternate may be to make its facilities available for public use. The decision to so utilize such private resources must be based on potential good for the whole community, certainly not in terms of bailing out those in financial straits. The plan is an opportunity for the entire sector of the community, public and private—not a solution for institutional problems.

## PLAN FOR FACULTY ACCOUNTABILITY:
## PASSAIC COUNTY COMMUNITY COLLEGE

ROBERT S. ZIMMER, *president, Passaic County Community College*

At Passaic County Community College, in Paterson, New Jersey, we believe that we cannot apply predetermined standards, clearly defined behavioral objectives, and tested material presentations to the student body, and at the same time apply subjective, personal, and/or hearsay forms of evidence in fixing faculty compensation, rank, and tenure. It is patently unfair to demand predetermined performance objectives of students and not of the faculty. Therefore, we developed a performance contract which defines, in behavioral terms, precisely what the teacher must do for retention, tenure, and promotion. This systems approach mandates well-defined performance specifications so that the desired outcome can be identified and evaluated. At the same time, it provides a pragmatic and an empirical means of modifying the initial objectives and recycling them through the system.

### Critical Decision Points

The first critical decision was made by the college trustees in accepting the concept of a performance contract for the faculty. The laymen on the board were sensitive to the fiscal pressures on higher education today and so were predisposed toward making faculty accountable and responsible. A performance contract joining faculty advancement and documented student learning seemed to fit the tone of the time.

Members of the personnel committee of the trustees first had to decide whether to have a one-year or a three-year initial faculty contract. A three-year contract admittedly provided more security; the faculty member was allowed that period of time, uninhibited by concerns of yearly employment, to develop a refined program of studies, with the opportunity to make mistakes without loss of face or employment. The advantage of an initial one-year contract was the obvious one of protecting the institution from a long-term financial commitment to a totally unsatisfactory faculty member, associated with development of effective programs of studies and related instructional strategies.

The application of performance specification for promotion as well as retention required considerable analysis of the existing state laws. The state laws governing community colleges in New Jersey specify a faculty member must be given tenure after three years; and a tenured faculty member can be removed from office only if there is clear evidence of his inadequacy. Such evidence, we concluded, could be provided by a performance contract. Efficiency is the essence of a performance contract; the contract provides the courts with an absolute measure of performance. The definition of the faculty member as one who designs, implements, manages, and evaluates learning experiences for "x" number of students provided the basic vehicle for the development of the contract. "Those who can teach more students more effectively" describes the rationale on which this contract is based. "More students" implies a numbers game. In an institution committed to the learning process, one measure of productivity obviously would be the numbers of students taught by the faculty. If this were the only criterion, there would be myriad opportunities for exploitation of the student body by the faculty and a prostitution of the learning process. With the qualifying phrase "more effectively," a necessary control is added. A qualitative measuring device became necessary. What would be an acceptable qualitative measure of the learning process? It was decided that the percentage of students successfully meeting the objectives of the course would be that measure. Again, unscrupulous individual faculty members could circumvent the system. However, this danger would be essentially avoided by the requirement that the objectives of all courses must be stated in verifiable terms of a behavioral change, thus predetermining the standards of a course. The balance of the hazard was eliminated by the addition of a college examiner who validates student learning, curriculum content, and instructional procedures—the base upon which faculty performance requirements rest; the essence of this process, however, is the verification of student achievement of the stated learning objectives of each course. As an internal auditor of the learning process, the examiner assured the degree of objectivity necessary for faculty acceptance and the success of the system.

The course objectives and their measurement have also been subjected to such external auditors as visiting consultants and public agencies (accrediting associations, state agencies, testing services). The creditability of the institution and the integrity of the administration and trustees throughout are critical factors. Arbitrary and capricious decisions affecting faculty retention and promotion would completely subvert the basic institutional philosophy. Only continual vigilance on the part of the trustees and administration can avoid the temptation to revert to traditional promotion practices, which may be only indirectly related to student learning.

**Results**

The inauguration of the systems approach at Passaic County Community College was done with the expectation of delivering better instruction more effectively to students; that is, more students would learn more effectively under this approach than any other that was available to us. The hard evidence on the success or failure of our approach is not in; it must accumulate for a little longer. We need at least three years to draw real conclusions. At that time, not earlier than 1975, the results of our efforts will be documented and available for publication.

One of the basic assumptions of the systems approach is that it is self-correcting. That is, by documenting the objectives of the course in behavioral terms, measuring them, and making decisions as to the effectiveness of the learning strategy, and the degree to which a given performance objective is satisfied, the instructor and the staff of the college can take corrective and modifying action to assure that the best learning techniques are used to attain the objectives that are appropriate for the course. Faculty are strongly encouraged to develop a variety of learning strategies. Their contracts specify at least two, and one learning strategy must be self-instructional. It is anticipated that as the behavioral objectives of a course are increasingly refined, additional strategies will be added, so that students can satisfy course requirements in a variety of ways. With the possibilities of change in strategy and in time element, many institutional changes are being forecast, many changes in physical plant, changes in the faculty support services, and changes in faculty and student roles. The day of the "professor" professing his discipline to a group of students will continue to diminish under our system. Faculty will be assuming more and more the role of managing instructional resources to assist students in mastering the behaviors, the performances, and/or the specifications of a given course. This is definitely a populist theory; this college is not elitist-oriented. The role of the faculty is to find ways in which students can learn, keeping in mind that students learn differently and at different rates of speed. The course manager will have to manage the resources at his disposal to bring the maximum number of students through the learning experiences toward the mastery of the objectives of the course.

## Articulation

In developing the new institution, we felt that the incoming staff had to accept the basic concepts and constraints of the innovation. Knowing and accepting the discipline of these parameters, the individual faculty member would then have much greater freedom of action, movement, and creativity within them.

The faculty were screened rather rigorously; they had to demonstrate that they had read prescribed works regarding behavioral objectives (Bloom, 1964, 1968; Zimmer, 1970) by writing and classifying their own objectives. A candidate became an active candidate for employment only upon submission of this evidence. Thus, we brought together a group of individuals who had committed themselves in more than a peripheral way to the proposed innovations. They demonstrated their skills in writing objectives, and directly and indirectly stated that they were accepting, or even embracing, the concepts upon which the college would function.

Our articulation with other institutions has been quite different. We had to sell our concepts in an area of conservative-traditional institutions of higher education, with gratifying results. The accrediting agencies have been more than supportive, as have our sister institutions within the state. All have been helpful and sympathetic, with great empathy for our institutional and systems problems. We think that some of them are envious of our opportunity to start a new institution with greater opportunities for innovation.

Our institutional articulation will be continued as our students move through our courses, earn credit, and start transferring to other institutions. As this occurs, we will be in a position to follow their problems and successes. Their performance specifications will be on record, so that as they transfer to other institutions we can compare their performance here with their performance at the receiving institution. The resulting comparisons will be a much better measure of what the student has accomplished than a catalog course description or the title on the typical college transcript. We anticipate that our students will be able to move with a great deal of ease into and through other institutions of higher education as they complete their work at Passaic County Community College.

## Steps in Developing the Plan

This type of systems approach to learning requires that the college (1) commit trustees to a cost-effective approach to the learning process; (2) select faculty who are philosophically committed to the approach; (3) provide in-service training for new and returning staff; (4) acquire resources essential to support the general and intensive requirement that faculty develop varied learning strategies; these resources would include (beyond the usual libraries, laboratories, and shops) autotutorial centers, learning resource centers, and computers for instructional purposes; (5) define faculty performance specification in contractual form; (6) provide for auditing of instructional performance; (7) anticipate problems and plan for continual review and refinement.

DENTISTRY EDUCATION AND RURAL VILLAGE
DEVELOPMENT:
UNIVERSIDAD DE SAN CARLOS DE GUATEMALA

WINSLOW R. HATCH, *chief of mission to Paraguay, United
Nations Development Program; formerly consultant, Organization of American States*

The program described here is a response to Guatemala's
urgent need to do something about a critical national problem. Actually, it is a supranational problem, for it is concerned with how
a country demonstrably and permanently improves the lot of its disadvantaged minorities. Despite the proportions and complexity of
the problem, the students and faculty of the college of dentistry of
San Carlos National University in Guatemala City have responded
with an educational program that has social and cultural overtones
but is justified largely on its educational merits. The Guatemalan
experience is related to the concepts of the "campus without walls"
and community and student involvement in the learning process.
The key figure in the Guatemalan program is Carlos Pomes, who
completed graduate studies at Northwestern University (see Pomes,
1968). Joining him and other members of the dental faculty are all
the majors in dentistry at the Universidad de San Carlos de Guatemala. Joining the dental students are some medical students and
students in social work, engineering, and nutrition. The central and
provincial governments are involved as are also some private
citizens.

The principles around which the program is built are external accountability; the advancement of the purposes of human
ecology; the conviction that dental (and medical) services must be
made available at a price the country can afford—which, for the
college, is a matter of professional responsibility; and the conviction
that the education provided, particularly since this is a Latin American program, must be task-oriented, with the desired behaviors
built into the task (see Hatch, 1974). These principles or convictions are seen as applying to both the campus and the extramural
program and are well developed by the college in its publications.

Specifically, the program has the following objectives: It gives students an opportunity to gain experience in the most difficult environment in which they will have to practice their dentistry. It exposes future dentists to the problems of oral health where they are greatest; namely, in the Indian village. It develops their capacity to resolve the problems of the community. It motivates students to see national problems in terms of their socioeconomic and cultural aspects. It enables students to identify the barriers that the environment offers to the exercise of their profession—barriers attributed to cultural, economic, and social characteristics. It forces students to acquire an understanding of social problems that relate to oral health. It forces the college to face up to the social and professional requirements in indigenous dentistry.

Some of the "learning tasks" required of the students in the college of dentistry are (1) to survey the mouths of school children in 130 Indian villages each year and to see to it that all acute dental problems are dealt with; (2) to set up private practices in these villages such that dental services are dispensed at a cost even the Indians can afford and at which the dentist can make a living (the dentist makes his living out of his low costs—that is, no rent, simple equipment, and the volume of his practice); (3) to improve the diet of the Indians by the diversification of their agriculture; (4) to improve their economy through the introduction of viable home industries; and (5) to do all of this through an education on and off campus that consciously tries to achieve the social and educational purposes described earlier.

## Program Description

Indoctrination into the program takes place principally in seminars given by graduating seniors returning from ten months in Indian villages. In these seminars, lasting several weeks, the graduates advise entering students, students in course, and faculty and administration. These seniors are the principal exponents of a teaching in which the passive memorization and regurgitation of facts is decried. Since the seniors have completed their fieldwork (chosen their villages, made their own arrangements, and worked out their own approaches), they are also expert in community involvement.

Much of the program design and content is credited to Pomes and his leadership in the dental faculty. As with most strong men, there seems to have been some jealousy inside and outside the college. Therefore, the enhancement and enlargement of the program usually had to come from students. Now the program is a solid, irreversible achievement with strong internal and external support.

For the entering student the program builds progressively toward the final year and the ten months' experience in the villages. Students learn about the dental problems of different Indian populations; they also learn how to use equipment that is not electrically powered but is light enough to carry by hand and simple enough to reduce costs. Their techniques similarly have to be adapted to the special and massive needs of their patients and their inability to pay very much—for example, a simple extraction costs 25 cents; a complex one, fifty cents. Usually, there is a dialect to master. There are also problems in basic education because the villagers are very ignorant and superstitious. It is also necessary for them to train paramedical aides from among the villagers and to design systems for distributing and controlling the distribution of drugs. Despite these problems, the long days they work, and their isolation, the students are not sorry for themselves but express pride and show exhilaration in their work.

### Evaluation

Although the program is only about ten years old, its achievements are already well documented by motion pictures and innumerable reports. A close reading of these reports shows a modesty on the part of the founders equal only to their dedication. One can say with confidence that the program has met effectively the problems typically encountered in student motivation. This was a particularly difficult problem because the students had to be persuaded that they would be better dentists for the experience; and they had to be willing to sacrifice a higher income and a plush office in the nation's capital. While the graduates from the program are among the country's best dentists, they have also given Guatemala something that the dentists (and medical professions) in the

United States have not provided—namely, dental (and medical)´ care that their patients typically can afford.

In addition to these pragmatic observations of the program's worth and impact, authorities responsible for it have devised an elaborate, technical system of measurements. It is too complex to take up fully here, but it involves use of several bipolar scaled axes. These axes deal with virtually all of the objectives described earlier, and their use is reflected in their designations: the dependent-independent axis, the analysis-synthesis axis, the factual-theoretical axis, the pedestrian-creativity axis, the social awareness–nonawareness axis. The activities measured include teaching and learning and performance on and off campus. Dental and community-development skills are also noted. From these axes a profile is developed. It is like an intellectual fingerprint of a student, teacher, or program element; and a numerical figure can be ascribed to the achievement.* Beyond this, an evaluation of each senior's year in the villages is made by periodic on-the-spot checks. Finally, the seniors spend three months evaluating the program.

## Productivity

The program has had notable success in producing short-range improvements in the dental health of villagers. The longer-range problems are more difficult to deal with, slow to correct, and difficult to appraise. But progress is clearly being made. The intangible positive consequences for the participating students and the people in the villages are, however, very real and very great—no matter how much still remains to be done.

A pragmatic measure of the program's success is that the colleges involved, largely by the efforts of their students, are among those the government supports most adequately. While other university programs are thought of as "communistic" and are therefore not supported, this program, which is communal, is not viewed as communistic but rather as the government's chief bulwark against communism.

Finally, all the parties involved realize, if in different de-

* The obvious relationship of this evaluation scheme and the *inter-active forces theory* of change in higher education should be noted.

grees, that the program cannot be considered sufficient until the economic base of the Indian communities is improved to the point where the causes of poor teeth and poor health are ameliorated. The staff and students are, accordingly, studying Peru's experience with Indian cooperatives and the successes achieved by the Otavalo Indians and the townspeople and teachers in Pujili, both in Ecuador. (For these and other programs, see *Programa Regional de Desarrollo Educativo*, 1971). This realization is an indication of the maturity of the program and of the students. The infusion of these additional elements will give the program a regional, even hemispherical, quality. As early as 1968–69, Dr. Pomes was making visits to dental and medical colleges in the United States responding to their invitations. Since then, whole teams of American dental faculties have traveled to Guatemala to learn more about the Indian village-development program. More recently Pomes' students are visiting this country expressly because of their experience in Guatemala and the growing interest among professional schools in the United States in their program. While affluent countries may be the last to get the message because they have more money to waste, they, too, seemingly will have to adopt these practices. What these affluent and more "developed" countries are missing can be seen in the faces of the Guatemalan students and the Indians with whom they work.

# VI

# Currents of
# Change

At least six major currents of change seem evident in American higher education today.

First of all, many institutions of higher education are pursuing new social objectives. Colleges and universities are accepting increased responsibility for the well-being of their communities. Several exhibits—including those on the College for Human Services, the Guatemalan program, Johns Hopkins, and the University Year for ACTION—describe new outreach programs of human service. Professional and paraprofessional programs are being developed in fields ranging from juvenile-court counseling and public-welfare casework to social therapy in mental hospitals. There is, in short, increased concern for the quality of life—for equal opportunity, improved intergroup and international relations, and education, among other values (Harris, 1973). While retaining allegiance to traditional academic values of cognitive intelligence and individual responsibility and achievement, colleges are devoting attention to such values as community, cooperation, and social responsibility.

A second change is the focus on learning rather than teaching. The fact that over half of the innovations described in this book have as their prime focus improvements in the learning process illustrates a national trend in higher education: one away from an emphasis on teaching and toward student learning. Until recently, the assumption has been that learning is inextricably linked with teaching and that psychological and fiscal support for the teacher automatically redounds to the benefit of the learner. But—as more and more educational research has shown, and as several of the exhibit cases illustrate—the correlation between teaching input and learning output is far from perfect. Thus, the focus is shifting from input to output—to behavioral objectives, to competency-based goals, to performance criteria. Statements of the objectives of a course or degree program are moving from "coverage" of a body of information to anticipated student skills—such as "The student will be able to . . ."

This shift in academic focus from teaching to learning parallels a larger shift beyond the campus: that of increased attention to the consumer in contrast to the producer. Undoubtedly the decrease in applications experienced by many institutions, together with the dissatisfaction and disenchantment expressed by many students, is hastening the impact of this larger value shift within higher education.

Another current of change is the separation of postsecondary functions. Traditionally the missions of instruction, research, and public service have been combined in the university; but developments (illustrated by the exhibits on the Oklahoma televised instructional system, the Regents External Degree, Empire State College, and the Dallas Public Library, among others) suggest the possible separation rather than the continued integration of these three classical functions of higher education in single institutions. The cultural cohesion which has united these academic missions in one setting is dissolving (Kuhns and Martorana, 1974); already a variety of research and public-service functions are being undertaken by nonacademic centers, and a similar fragmentation of the instructional mission is occurring through the open university, the credentialing agency, and related innovations. Just as learning may not result from teaching *per se*, so without ever attending a class meeting, seeing an advisor, talking with peers, or exploring a college library, a student may earn an associate or a baccalaureate degree. Not only may course credit and degrees be granted in complete isolation from any instructional process; counseling and socialization may be entirely abandoned as the most easily expended elements of the instructional mission.

Questions can justifiably be asked about the similarity between this learning and that gained in a setting that combines teaching, counseling, and student socialization; and further research will test current theories about the potential of independent learning (Moore, 1973). But there is no question that the fragmentation of these educational functions can occur, for it is occurring now; and there seems no question that this fragmentation will have major consequences both for student learning and for institutional planning.

Along with this separation of functions, many institutions are giving up the requirement that all work creditable toward their degrees must occur after their students matriculate. Credit by examination and credit for previous experiential education are both illustrated graphically by Minnesota Metropolitan State College in Chapter Three. After some initial hesitation at colleges and universities, the idea of nationally recognized college-level examinations has achieved widespread acceptance, and guidelines are now available to assist colleges in assigning credit on the basis of these examinations.

Determining credit for experiential education, and particularly *ex post facto* for experience, presents a more difficult problem, as illustrated at the College for Human Services (Chapter Two) and Empire State College (Chapter Three) and by Houle in his volume on *The External Degree* (1973). But here, too, credits and degrees are no longer being equated merely with certain blocks of classroom instruction but instead with student competence and performance. For lack of a better measure, the criterion of elapsed time spent in the classroom assumed until now a role of major importance in defining academic degrees that were acceptable to licensing and accrediting agencies, future employers, and students themselves. Institutions seeking to redefine criteria for degrees are faced with the problem posed by the stigma of "degree mills" and outright fraudulent institutions that offer degrees on no other criterion than the payment of money; but the best answer to this problem seems to lie in the direction of rigorous use of performance-based evaluations of student competence and achievement.

In addition, at some colleges degree programs may be subject to student definition, with appropriate advisory assistance; and institutions employing a contract approach to learning continuously involve students in drafting learning contracts with their professors. Sometimes, the attainment of the degree is more important to students than the experiences involved in gaining the degree, because the degree is perceived as a key to social and economic power. Thus, it is unlikely that students will be permitted to participate in degree decisions without faculty supervision and veto power. But there is some evidence that student interest only in a degree, rather than in education as such, may be declining— as witness data from national studies indicating that dropping in and out of college is becoming a way of life for many young people —hardly the behavior of those steadfastly seeking a degree (Carnegie Commission, 1971). Presently, degrees rather than the knowledge they represent are often necessary prerequisites to employment (Ashby, 1973). This emphasis on degrees may change, however, as knowledge itself becomes the primary credential for employment and success (Bell, 1973).

Another current of change is in the direction of structural flexibility. Quite evidently a general concern now exists in higher education about institutional rigidity and how to combat it. Examples abound. For instance, prior to the advent of self-paced instruction, learning for mastery (Bloom, 1968), and flexible calendar arrangements (Kuhns, 1974), all students taking a given course were expected to begin together at the first class meeting and end together at the final examination, regardless of the varying rates of progress made by the different students. The exhibit cases show an increasing incidence of self-paced instruction; and in some institutions students may now enter a course at any time during the academic year. A related phenomenon is the widespread move toward giving students both the privilege and the responsibility for designing their own courses and degree programs. As noted above, the contract system of learning demands a considerable degree of student initiative in setting objectives and planning strategies for their implementation; but it offers students programs keyed to their own needs.

Another element in this structural flexibility is increased fusion of formerly discrete levels of education and training. For example, at the Center for Allied Health Careers at Johns Hopkins (Chapter Four) various levels of medical paraprofessionals and professionals all concentrate on a common body of knowledge at the same time. Such multilevel simultaneous education is also illustrated at Oakton Community College (Chapter Two). In this approach, skillful instructors with appropriate auxiliary equipment may serve as learning facilitators in a language laboratory for students representing as many as five- or six-year differences in their level of language competence, or in a mathematics class for students with an equally wide range of mathematical skills. The principle in both institutions is the same: with appropriate instructional materials, students with varying backgrounds and levels of previous education can learn together rather than in the traditionally separate classes. This juxtaposition of students also encourages peer instruction, which in many cases is as educational for the student teacher as for the learner. Not since the days of the one-room schoolhouse has the age-graded rigidity of the instructional pattern in colleges and schools been under such scrutiny and attack. As President Hall of Empire State noted in Chapter Three, "While college faculties have always endorsed the principle of *knowledge change* based upon research findings . . . in matters of *organizational change* faculties have been notoriously conservative." The evidence from Heiss (1973), Levine and Weingart (1973), and the Cornell University Center for the Improvement of Undergraduate Education (1974) indicates that although Hall may well be correct, toleration for increased fluidity of curricular and other organizational arrangements is growing.

A fifth major current of change is the emphasis on learning from direct experience. Early in the history of higher education, students used primary sources rather than compiled texts and acquired much of their professional knowledge by following the craft of the practicing doctors, lawyers, and ministers who taught them. In a number of the exhibits in earlier chapters may be seen a trend back to direct experience and to "action learning" through work-study, cooperative education, internships, off-campus study, and other forms of experiential education. Because this education occurs in the real world, which the student must be prepared to meet, such programs not only have interdisciplinary features—such as combining elements of academic disciplines with technical or professional subjects—but also integrate cognitive, affective, and psychomotor learning. In his report on Empire State College, President Hall explained why such action learning until recently has not been deemed worthy of credit; and even today, colleges and universities granting credit for such learning often have an upper limit of hours permitted toward a degree. But clearly the trend is in the direction of increased integration of classroom and experience and the redefinition of degrees to include experience.

Finally, there is a drift toward systemization, where two or more colleges interrelate, either officially or informally. This drift is illustrated in the previous chapters by the cooperation between Union College and Union County Technical Institute in New Jersey, whereby students are able to pursue both technical and liberal arts education (Chapter Five); by the cross-registration of students at Westminster and William Woods Colleges (Chapter Five); by Oklahoma's Talkback Television program (Chapter Three); and by Johns Hopkins' cooperation with high schools and public community colleges in its community-based medical-education program (Chapter Four).

Although this trend toward interinstitutional systems is most apparent among public institutions, almost no college or university, private or public, is truly autonomous any more. Patterson (1973) reports that over eight hundred institutions of higher education now participate in formal consortia for academic purposes, such as cross-registration, library specialization, and cooperative programs; and if such other groupings as state systems, interstate arrangements, and nonacademic associations were to be included, the number would include almost every institution. A survey of independent junior colleges and of state systems of public community colleges corroborates the readiness of these institutions to enter into group arrangements and to cooperate in the use of their institutional resources (Martorana and others, 1975).

Various categorical aid programs of the federal government (such as grants for comprehensive statewide coordination and for improving certain classes of institutions) have actively encouraged interinstitutional cooperation as a way of extending scarce resources and upgrading the offerings of developing institutions; and despite problems resulting from regimentation, more systematic statewide coordination can be expected. The trend toward providing fiscal support to students, as in the Higher Education Amendments of 1972, however, may cause increased competition. Martorana (1974) points out that the provision for systematic statewide coordination also may be divisive; increasing evidence indicates that tensions resulting from collectivism among colleges, whether on a voluntary basis or as a result of official governmental actions, will increase (Patterson, 1974).

Central to all of these trends is increased emphasis on the academic consumers rather than on the producer. Much evidence in the exhibit chapters indicates that colleges are increasingly student-oriented. This orientation is closely linked to the condition of the academic marketplace, where a buyer's market now exists among students. Currently institutions are competing fiercely for students to fill the spaces resulting from earlier overextensions in staff and facilities; and some important innovations for serving the perceived needs of students, such as systems approaches to learning, are being adopted in part as a survival tactic as well as because of their effectiveness. The relatively new federal policy of giving financial aid directly to students rather than to institutions can be expected to reinforce this tendency to cater to the expressed needs of students.

Two other conclusions seem justified from the cases in earlier chapters and other studies: much of the innovation in American colleges still is piecemeal, often little related to institutional goals; and little of it is adequately evaluated.

Regarding the first of these conclusions, an ad hoc approach to academic change was reasonable, perhaps, when continuing growth could be expected to hide past mistakes. But in the steady state likely to characterize the academic community for the rest of the 1970s, a more systematic, thoughtful, global approach—oriented toward the achievement of clearly defined institutional objectives— appears to be more likely to assure institutional survival.

As part of a more systematic approach to innovation, more adequate evaluation is mandatory. The evidence from the case studies in this volume demonstrates that academic innovation too frequently is planned on the basis of guesswork and hunch and that provision seldom is made for evaluating the results of the change on more than an informal assessment. The deficiency seems to be not with innovators alone; they themselves are concerned about the lack of a firm research base for planning, managing, implementing, and evaluating change. Instead, the deficiency seems to be in the typical level of financial support for innovation that is available. As already noted, about a third of the changes described in previous chapters were aided by federal or foundation funds; but the rest were being pursued essentially without outside support. It is a truism that planning and evaluative research cost money. But when research is an integral part of an experiment—for example, at Corning Community College—the results are most often positive and helpful. Traditionally faculty want evidence, and rightly so. Ongoing institutional research can do much to provide an evidentiary base for proposed changes. Many colleges that would prefer the careful planning and evaluation of change are usually induced to allocate the necessary dollars elsewhere. Outside funding agencies can help assure systematic planning and evaluation by specifying these activities as a requirement in their grants.

# VII

# Guidelines for
# Change Leaders

Earlier chapters gave examples of how the processes of change were initiated, directed, and managed in relation to specific innovations. In those chapters, only the most global strategies for effecting change were categorized—strategies such as creating new campus-based or noncampus institutions, organizing satellite operations as part of an ongoing institution, or attempting to alter the traditional program of such an institution. But innovators, as catalysts of change—that is, as stimulators—or as the administrators and managers of change, need to formulate and execute numerous actions within these several alternative approaches. Change agents and managers must deal with specific questions of strategy and tactics in order to accomplish their goals.

A strategy is an overall plan of action for achieving a goal. (A comprehensive and pointed discussion of the role and function of educational strategies and of the essential elements of such strategies appears in Faure and others, 1973, chap. 7.) Thus, a strategy for innovation in a college or university, as in any other enterprise, starts with concepts of goals (what is to be achieved) and proceeds to the question of overall design (how can these goals be gained with assurance and efficiency). Within every adequate strategy there needs to be what the military analysts refer to as "room for maneuver"—latitude that permits variation in the techniques used in effecting the strategy and in the timing of the use of these techniques. Tactics are the specific actions taken to implement chosen strategies. Both strategies and tactics imply movement toward the achievement of predetermined goals. Strategies are the more encompassing plans for action; within the limits set by the goals strategies provide the broad parameters for action. Tactics are ways of carrying out strategies. Tactics are trial and error phenomena; they are expendable. If a tactic does not support a given strategy, it must be abandoned and another tried in its place. Most importantly, strategies allow change leaders to acquire control over the enterprise led, particularly control of the initiative for change of direction and deployment of resources; tactics are simply means toward implementing the strategy that is being followed. To use the analogy of constructing a building, the finished building is the goal; the blueprint is the strategy; and the tools used and steps taken in the process of construction are the tactics.

Various combinations of overall strategies and specific tactics were obvious in the previous cases of innovation; but some selected combination of strategies and tactics may prove more advantageous than others in directing certain types of innovation. Changes that aim at increased participation by students and faculty members in decisions affecting their own work may not best be implemented through strategies and tactics limited to administrative directives, just as innovations that aim at more systematic planning and experimentation can probably best be achieved through systematic planning and experimentation themselves.

## Strategies for Change

A considerable body of literature has developed about strategies for organizational change at large (see, for example, Beckhard, 1969) and in educational organizations in particular (for example, Holm, 1972). The following strategies are drawn from these and other cited publications and from the exhibits in earlier chapters. Although not all of these strategic approaches are equally acceptable or recommended, all have some positive and some negative features, depending on how they are used and the general organizational context in which they are employed.

*Low-profile action.* The simplest and often the best strategy (particularly when extensive opposition is expected) is to deemphasize the importance of the change and to emphasize instead its relation to traditional procedures. Maintaining, by design, a low-profile posture in effect becomes a subtle plan whereby the change leader retains control of the nature and direction of the change desired. By adopting such a strategy, academic innovators can lessen opposition by persuading others that the change is in reality a *reform*—an effort to return the institution to its true goals and to make the institution more successful at accomplishing its traditional purposes—rather than a *transformation,* aimed at changing the institution into something else or deflecting it from its original aims. Thus, a new teaching technique can be championed not as a revolutionary alternative to outmoded and unsatisfactory techniques but instead as an already widely accepted means of fulfilling more satisfactorily an institution's long-standing educational objectives.

*Systematic experimentation.* "Systematic experimentation is a radical new strategy of social reform. The key word is 'systematic.' 'Experiment' has been loosely used in recent years as a synonym for 'new' or 'innovative.' Government and foundations have promoted hundreds of 'experimental' programs, but no one has been following a strategy of systematic experimentation. Indeed, the strategy of the 1960s is more aptly described as 'random innovation'" (Rivlin, 1971, p. 87). The evidence from previous chapters and from higher education generally confirms Rivlin's complaint: only in a few cases can it be said that truly systematic and experimental procedures have been used in planning and testing academic changes. Among the twenty examples cited, only the confluent-education program of Corning Community College and to some extent the three-year baccalaureate at Geneseo involved some control-group and experimental-group research. This rigorous approach to planning and evaluating change seems particularly natural for academic institutions.

*Participant involvement versus power coercion.* In terms of authority, participant involvement contrasts with power-coercive strategies in assuming that "change will be most effective when each participant makes a personal commitment to change" and that commitment is best gained "through cooperation in the decision-making process and through programs of reeducation" in which participants clarify and, where appropriate to them, change their value orientation toward the proposed change. Conversely, power-coercive strategies "assume power to be located in the hands of a few, e.g., 'management,' who achieve change by manipulating organizational conditions such as rewards, sanctions, sources of information, and relationships among the participants" (Sagen, 1972, p. 21). Here the evidence from higher education indicates that participant involvement, rather than power coercion, is typical of academic innovation; the evidence also seems to indicate that the more participant involvement, the more successful the adoption of the innovation.

*Creation of demand.* Since colleges and universities are essentially social-purpose institutions, one way to cause them to change is to create a new demand within the society they serve. New demands generate a call for new practices. It is important to distinguish clearly between a need and a demand and to find ways to convert needs into demands. A condition of need can exist for a long time without a concomitant demand for action to meet it. Until the perceived need turns into demands, little or no organizational change is likely to occur because there are no pressures, no interactive forces, to cause the changes. Blocker, Bender, and Martorana (1974) suggest that in order to set such pressures to action, responsible persons and agencies need to enter into a process of political action within the organization, between it and other external agencies, or in both arenas. In other words, change agents and managers need to activate the possible interactive forces on behalf of the change desired; the strategy of creating demand does this by changing the institutional setting and thereby forcing new organizational responses.

Since demands are basically the articulation of the wants of particular groups in the society or organization, the strategy of modifying institutional settings typically involves dealing with such groups or their spokesmen. If the institution's response to their demands is lacking or inappropriate, those expressing the demand will either abandon the institution or generate more intense pressure upon it to be responsive. Thus, in the face of a generally unresponsive higher educational community to the need for new human-services personnel, leadership of the College for Human Services (Chapter Two) joined forces with the employers of such workers in New York City to create a new response, a new college. In contrast, the developments at Union College (Chapter Five) were guided to generate new attitudes toward interinstitutional cooperation, and relatively little structural change within the institution itself was necessary to effect the needed accommodation to public needs and demands.

*Development of legitimacy.* Legitimacy in higher education operations can come through laws and official policies; through action by regional and professional accreditation associations; or through individual standouts among the faculty (such as a Nobel Prize winner) or other persons, associations, organizations of high and widespread prestige. Part of the strategy which permitted embarkation on the Empire State College and external-degree innovations in New York State, for example, was the acquisition of the endorsement of the prestigious Carnegie Corporation. This endorsement, because of the legitimizing effect it produced, was a factor perhaps as important to the overall strategy of the innovations as the later tactical negotiations of budgets for Carnegie support.

*Creation of power blocs.* All organizations and units within organizations seek to develop support and reinforcement of their efforts by identifying and associating themselves with others believed capable of rendering positive influence on their behalf. The creation of a power bloc seeking to accomplish a common goal is a strategy as old as man. Several of the innovations described in the exhibit chapters show evidence of this strategy as one means of enhancing success. Illustrations are Oklahoma Talkback Television (Chapter Three), where a strong coalition occurred between the business and higher educational interests; the program for dental training in Guatemala (Chapter Five), where governmental-political interests joined with the university; and the community health-care program at Johns Hopkins (Chapter Four), where educational and community groups joined hands.

*Control of internal organization.* Another strategic approach, flexible grouping of organizations or subunits within an organization, is a variant to the power-bloc strategy, except that it is used to counteract a threat or other action considered to be against the interests of those coming into the alliance. Alliances center around issues—for example, the issue of whether a new comprehensive community college should be established in Union County. In that case, as reported in Chapter Five, Union College and a local technical institute joined forces; to prevent the possible emergence of a competing institution, they initiated an innovative program that was more compatible with their individual institutional goals and traditional operations.

*Control of communication.* The strategy that is built upon control of the information about a proposed change is difficult to illustrate because it is seldom used in isolation and also because it is difficult to document. At its best, this strategy spotlights and dramatizes the fact that the innovation is underway and merits attention of all interested parties; at its worst, it distorts information by disseminating only what is favorable to a proposed innovation and suppressing that which is negative. This practice is generally recognized, widely acknowledged, and often expected. We do not suggest, however, that any of the exhibit innovations have failed to have full information released; some, in fact, are seeking to get all the publicity possible.

## Tactics for Implementation

Like strategies, most tactics have both positive and negative connotations. For ethical reasons, therefore, some are less desirable to use as techniques for effecting change. The examples here are drawn in part from our own observations and in part from the observations of others (Hefferlin, 1972; Blocker, Bender, and Martorana, 1974).

*Appreciation of timing.* Correct timing is of undeniable importance in many innovations. Mayhew, in fact, identifies "timing of the change in relation to the life of the institution" as one of the necessary conditions of success in educational innovation (1973a, p. 64). Timing involves forecasting, as outlined by Bell (1973), and, as indicated in the next chapter, assessing the trend of forces impinging on the innovation.

*Obtaining an overview.* The effective change agent or change manager, whether faculty member or administrator, should be able to perceive the relationship between the proposed change and other aspects of the campus environment, to view the interlocking problems of the entire institution, and to be concerned with the total institution. In this sense, a relationship may exist between the success of an academic innovation and the breadth of view held by the proponents of the change, with the more successful innovations propounded by those with the most global and perceptive view.

*Determining obstacles.* One outcome of obtaining a broad overview of an institution is a sense of the obstacles most likely to interfere with the proposed change. These obstacles must be overcome or avoided, just as objections and criticisms must be met or deflected. The change managers working to develop the University Year for ACTION program at Pepperdine University (Chapter Four) noted a very common phenomenon, that the faculty was conservative, particularly with respect to departmental prerogatives and requirements for the major. Another kind of obstacle was identified at Governors State University (Chapter Two), where the faculty came to realize that governance is not an end in itself "but a means to serve educational purposes" and that the pursuit of particular objectives might serve abstract principles but prove to be an obstacle in serving the clientele's needs.

*Providing reassurance.* Change managers can avoid unnecessary opposition if they are clear about their ideas and their activities. Faculty orientation, particularly for new staff members, is a common form of communication to provide reassurance. At Oakton Community College (Chapter Two) every new faculty member participates in activities planned to acquaint him with the goals of the college and guidelines for their implementation, such as a deemphasis of learning for grades and an accentuation of learning for mastery. Sometimes reassurance through communication will be provided by groups external to the institution; at Minnesota Metropolitan (Chapter Three), for example, a widely respected civic group, with several hundred citizen members, first studied and then issued a report just as the legislature was considering the chancellor's proposal for a new kind of urban college for new kinds of students.

*Building on existing concerns.* Some self-study committees get off on the wrong foot by trying first of all to rewrite the opening page of the college catalog. Much of the educational philosophy at Simon's Rock (Chapter Two) came from a recognition that educational structure, nationally, has not kept pace with the rate at which young people are achieving social and emotional maturity. In the Oklahoma system of higher education (Chapter Three) an existing concern—that the strongest program offered at any one institution should be made available to students of all institutions— led to a plan for a network of closed-circuit microwave communication.

*Avoiding rejection.* At Colorado College (Chapter Five)' and Pepperdine University (Chapter Four), change managers avoided rejection by proposing the changes for only an experimental period, after which the innovative program was to be evaluated. In a somewhat different situation, the change managers at Corning Community College (Chapter Five) deliberately allowed the plans for confluent education to evolve slowly, so that staff members could discover that it was different from sensitivity training; their disapproval of sensitivity training could have led them to reject the concept of confluent education.

*Respecting the past.* The change managers associated with the Dallas Library's Independent Study Project (Chapter Three) realized that unless the colleges in the area were willing to accept credit earned through the CLEP tests, such credit would be of little advantage to independent-study participants. The change managers working to effect cross-registration at Westminster and William Woods Colleges (Chapter Five) were aware that they were dealing with deeply entrenched academic and social values of not one but two traditional institutions, and that the faculties feared "watering down the curriculum" and the dampening of open discussion by the cross-registration of members of the opposite sex. In such situations, change managers should try to be as traditional as possible in implementing change.

*Persuading the opposition.* The tactic of convincing opponents and neutrals that a particular course of action is appropriate for them and/or for the community or society at large, is evident in the story of several of the innovations discussed in this volume. For example, Simon's Rock (Chapter Two) found it necessary to convince the regional accrediting agency that it was indeed a college. The proposal to adopt the modular calendar at Colorado College (Chapter Five) was debated formally and informally for nearly a year, during which time both the supporters and those in opposition seemed to gain strength. The tactic of persuasion convinced enough of the opposition to permit a trial of the innovation, and in time many of their objections disappeared as most advantages claimed for the plan came to fruition.

*Confronting the opposition.* Confrontation, in which literally or symbolically the position or well-being of the opponents of the desired change is threatened, appears in a few of the case exhibits. At the College for Human Services (Chapter Two), for example, the cooperating author reports that "after a long struggle in which every facet of the institution participated, the charter battle was won." During that struggle the college sometimes adopted a show-down or confrontation position to overcome opposition by staff members working for the Regents. At Johnston College (Chapter Four), the creation of the cluster college within the parent university "generated a new source of competition and conflict" for the university, much of which has been ameliorated during the several maturation stages of this innovation.

*Compromise and co-opting.* Through compromise and co-optation, opposing groups can find a common ground and induce change into the system which is gradual rather than violent. At Westminster and William Woods Colleges (Chapter Five), for example, the faculty and staff had to work out numerous points of difficulty, such as college calendars, credit policies, daily class schedules, transportation, and departmental permissions, in order to effect a successful cross-registration plan. The Geneseo three-year baccalaureate innovation utilized elements of the co-optation technique in at least two instances: in getting special designation as the locus for this experiment within the SUNY system and in the resolution of the conflict over admissions criteria when the minority view finally prevailed.

*Selecting personnel for decision-making positions.* Selecting decision makers involves placing people on boards, committees, commissions, and other decision-making groups. When the planning committee was set up for the three-year baccalaureate program at Geneseo (Chapter Four), this group was "heavily weighted with full professors and department chairmen," an action which "fully engaged those with influence and power." At Passaic Community College (Chapter Five) the only faculty selected were those who were philosophically committed to goals of the college, and who were capable of implementing these goals through academic management by objectives.

*Using "trial balloons."* In the Coast Community College District (Chapter Five) and at Geneseo and Pepperdine (Chapter Four), possible reactions to the innovative program were tested before a firm decision was made. At Geneseo, administrative and faculty representatives of selected units were invited by SUNY central administration and the Carnegie Corporation to a three-day meeting. At Pepperdine, the president and officials of other area schools were first approached with the plan.

*Using a front man.* Use of a front man is another tactic for testing reactions and planting ideas. As an illustration, when the UYA program was being explored at Pepperdine (Chapter Four), the chairman of the communications arts department, a highly respected faculty member, went before the departmental council and the credits committee to outline the UYA program and the necessary academic procedures. The program was approved by both committees on an experimental basis.

*Carrying out hidden agenda.* An oblique approach to a subject, to disguise latent objectives or to short-circuit an idea or an opponent, seems to be a part of the procedure used in some of the exhibit cases. With respect to the three-year baccalaureate at Geneseo (Chapter Four), for example, the cooperating author identifies several motives for the development of this program, some of which might well qualify as "hidden agendas." To illustrate, Geneseo wanted "to find an institutional role that would prevent the college from becoming primarily a transfer institution for community college graduates"; some SUNY central administrators "saw the time-shortened program as an economical way to handle

increased numbers of students without committing additional resources"; some local administrators "may also have seen the opportunity to establish an innovative program that would be an asset in
the competition for limited funds and students"; and, finally, some
students also indicated a desire "to avoid certain subjects in typical
freshman core or distribution programs."

*Outflanking the opposition.* Outflanking movement, going
around the oppositional forces, is clearly a maneuver utilized in
some of the exhibit chapters. At the College for Human Services
(Chapter Two), for example, an attempt was made to control the
environment in order to create the kind of change desired. That is,
by making contractual commitments with participating community-
service agencies, the college solved potential employment problems
for students and graduates, who might otherwise experience dis-
crimination because of their unorthodox educational background.
The change managers at Empire State (Chapter Three) apparently
employed this tactic to avoid the charge that their program did not
contain the elements required for a college degree. As the cooperating author states, "unlike external-degree programs which have
hypothesized a standard curriculum, then created learning materials and examinations to enable the student to pursue and
demonstrate competency in that program, Empire State College has
undertaken the complex task of redefining the meaning and substance of a college degree."

# VIII

═══════════════════════════════════════

# Interactive Forces
of Change

The aim of this book is not to duplicate the work of other students on academic change nor merely to give examples of the content and processes of change now underway in American higher education. Instead, a major purpose is to provide personnel involved in these processes of change with a conceptual framework within which they can plan, project, and implement successful change. This "perceptual gestalt" for administrators, faculty members, trustees, and other decision makers focuses on the interacting forces which help or hinder the implementation of any innovation. We call this concept an *interactive forces theory*. With it, innovators can evaluate the progress of any particular change, monitor how well particular tactics and strategies are working, predict the likely outcome of these tactics and strategies in light of the multitude of forces impinging on the innovation, judge when the innovation is in danger, and take remedial action to assure its implementation.

## Theories as Tools

A theory may be defined as a coherently organized set of interrelated propositions which explain or assist in explaining a given subject. One of the most important functions of theories is the elimination of extraneous data so that the items under consideration may be illuminated and examined more adequately. Schon (1967, pp. 22–23) illustrates this function by comparing a detailed photograph and a simple drawing of the same subject. A photograph, he points out, can contain "too much information to permit identification of the object. Elimination of a good deal of it (in the line drawing) permits identification. . . . The function of . . . theory is to reduce the situation to one we can handle— that is, take account of, explain, and predict." Parsons and Platt make a similar point in discussing their work on the American university: "The study will attempt to be accurate with respect to relevant matters of fact, but it will also select facts by the use of a . . . theoretical scheme" (1973, p. 8).

The major test of scientific theories is their ability to predict the course of events. In theories of change, this means accurate prediction about the causes, forces, and outcomes of change. Structural-functional theorists, such as Talcott Parsons (1951), view social systems as continuing series of human action and reaction occurring within a complex of societally defined roles played by individuals with diverse needs and value standards. They contend that if behavior patterns are relatively repetitive, by definition the social system is internally stable and in equilibrium; and they concentrate on strains within social systems that may upset equilibrium and result in structural change of the system itself. By and large, sociological theorists have concentrated on large-scale systems and on major strains, such as class differences, cultural disparities, economic antagonisms, ideological antitheses, and other social differences that threaten social equilibrium.

There has been much less research into the relatively subtler and more muted forms of disjunction occurring within relatively homogeneous groupings, and thus there are correspondingly fewer assumptions about the sources of tension and the origins of competition and conflict in this kind of milieu. . . .

One example of this sort of milieu is a college or university. A university is, in theory, an intellectual community in which hostility and conflict are at a minimum. The actual state of affairs, as any knowing observer can report, is usually somewhat different [Wilson, 1972, p. 220].

A number of scholars have produced useful theoretical works for predicting change in such institutions as colleges and universities. A pioneer in the field of change was Kurt Lewin (1935), who based his "field theory" on differences he perceived between the conceptual approaches of Aristotle and Galileo. According to Lewin, quasi-stationary equilibrium occurs in a social situation when the forces which tend to strengthen a standard of behavior (for example, a particular academic tradition or expectation) are equal to those which tend to lower that standard. The level of conduct can be changed "by adding forces in the desired direction, or by diminishing opposing forces" (1961, p. 236). Such changes involve a three-step process: "unfreezing, moving, and freezing of a level" (p. 237).

George Levinger uses Lewin's ideas in analyzing the resolution of conflict—almost inevitably a concomitant of any change effort:

The conception that behavior is determined by forces or fields of forces lends itself readily to an analysis of conflict situation. . . . If we consider that the person at any given moment has the possibility of locomoting in the direction of many different regions, then any particular action is the resultant of some implicit resolution of conflict. . . . Lewin defined psychological conflict as a situation where the forces acting on the person are opposite in direction and about equal in strength. We shall use the terms "plus," "positive valence," and "approach" in reference to the existence of forces directed *toward* a given region. Similarly, the term "minus," "negative valence," and "avoidance" will refer to forces *away from* some region [1961, p. 244].

Stearns (1955) has applied Lewin's theory to decision making within the schools, as shown in Figure 1.

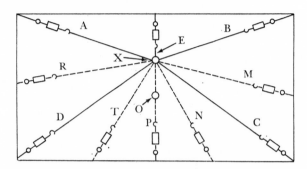

FIGURE 1. Forces impinging on a decision (after Stearns, 1955).

Suppose the position X is an inadequate school building which we wish to correct by the erection of a new building, bringing us to the desired position O. . . . Force E is the direct opposition of a taxpayers group. . . . A, which is an indirect pull away from the objective, could be the influence of parents who send their children to nonpublic schools, and B could be the influence of an industrial group pulling with the taxpayers on costs, but favoring the public schools over the independent schools on the grounds of a better vocational preparation program. The strong force P pulling directly for the new school would be the parents of public school children. C could be organized labor pulling indirectly for the public schools against the industrial group and the independent schools. D could be the indirect influence of real estate interests. . . . T and N could be any number of new forces, such as a newspaper influence, interests of organized minority groups, veterans and civic organizations whose indirect influence could be attracted toward the schools if properly appealed to [Stearns, 1955, p. 11].

Applying Lewin's three-stage theory to this case, the present balance of forces would need to be "unfrozen" by a series of actions to permit erection of the new school building, with the new balance of forces refrozen after the decision to proceed with construction is made.

Hodgkinson (1971, pp. 3–4) warns that models such as Lewin's may suggest that change is linear and predictable because it is viewed as the result of the application "of certain forces of certain strengths," when this is in fact not the case. Models which take into account the *interaction* of forces—their interplay of support or opposition—can avoid this simplistic assumption. Their analogy within the physical sciences might best be represented by tension-level experiments in physics.

The interactive forces theory of change developed in this chapter grows out of structural-functional theory, with its concern for the equilibrium of social institutions, and out of Lewinian field theory. It aims to help innovators objectively anticipate the relative strength of the various forces interacting on an innovation at each stage of its development and to use judgments about the strength of these forces as a guide in bringing to bear the maximum effect of all positive forces while simultaneously minimizing the cumulative effect of negative forces. By anticipating the potential relative influence of pro and con forces, planners can simulate the chances for successful implementation of any proposed change, and identify those alternative paths which would lead most directly to a desired goal. In brief, its use should facilitate better choices in the selection of educational innovations.

## Elements of the Theory

The interactive forces theory classifies forces for change in higher education as *personal, extrapersonal,* or *goal hiatus* forces. *Personal* forces are of three kinds: decision makers, people influential in the institution and its environment (such as presidents and deans, chancellors of state systems, individual officials of boards or commissions or a faculty senate); implementors (such as administrators when they are carrying out decisions in contrast to making decisions, faculty, and other academic professionals like business managers and librarians); and consumers (such as students, alumni, parents, legislators, the more advanced levels of educational institutions, and citizens at large). *Extrapersonal* forces include tangible influences (such as facilities, land, and equipment) and intangible ones (such as policies, traditions, trends, and laws ranging from affirmative-action regulations to collective-bargaining legislation). When forces move beyond the influence of single individuals, they are transposed from personal to extrapersonal forces and must be reckoned with as such. Thus, the voting behavior of individual faculty members is a personal force, but when the faculty establish an official faculty policy by vote, this policy becomes an extrapersonal force: an element impinging on proposals for change independent of the votes of individual faculty.

*Goal hiatus* refers to the discrepancy between the aspiration toward a particular institutional goal and the achievement of this goal. The value structure of any institution such as a college includes an informal and a formal ranking of goals, which results in a hierarchy of aspirations or priorities in the institution. We use two terms to describe the crucial force for innovation that results from the operation of the value structure in an institution: goal aspiration is the level of performance at which the institution would like to be; goal achievement is the level of performance at which the institution is. At any given time, then, the gap between the two levels is termed *goal hiatus,* which is thus a function or result of the aspiration/achievement ratio. For example, the hiatus at Union College in New Jersey (described in Chapter Five) between the aspiration of avoiding the emergence of a competing community college and the initial achievement of this goal was so great that it provided momentum at Union for its unusual interinstitutional arrangement with Union County Technical Institute and for Union efforts to get recognition of this arrangement in New Jersey statutes.

Institutional goals may be rated by individuals on such forms as the Institutional Goals Inventory (Educational Testing Service) and the Survey of Educational Needs (Center for Improved Education, Battelle Institute) to develop a hierarchy of institutional goal aspirations or priorities. Similarly, the degree of accomplishment of these aspirations can also be rated to form a hierarchy of goal achievement. The resulting hiatus between aspiration and achievement complements the personal and extrapersonal forces mentioned earlier and forms the third major category of influence affecting innovation.

Change is driven or energized by the result or effect of all interactive forces: personal, extrapersonal, and goal hiatus. From this the interactive forces theory develops a series of postulates as follows:

1. These three forces are identifiable, separable, and describable, and their individual impact on an innovation in both strength and direction (either negative or positive) is to some extent predictable.

2. These forces interact in ways which tend to reinforce or cancel their effect on the viability of the innovation; hence the label *interactive.*

3. Academic innovations, like other changes, display an identifiable growth or maturation pattern—in effect, a "life cycle" of developmental stages resulting from the interplay of forces over a period of time. This continuum can be divided into five finite developmental stages: *exploration, formulation, trial, refinement,* and *institutionalization.* The *exploration* stage in the life cycle of an innovation is marked by discussion, explanation, and conceptualization. Issues are clarified and elements of potential input, process, and output are identified. Objectives of the innovation are specified, including their relationship to institutional goals. This stage extends from the first awareness of the innovation to the first official action sanctioning an effort in this direction. The *formulation* stage is characterized by information-gathering about the elements and issues identified during the exploration stage. Alternative courses of action are studied, including that of abandoning the embryonic innovation. Costs, constraints, and potential resources are defined. The formulation stage ends when a decision is made to try the innovation. The *trial* stage is a pilot operation limited in time and scope but otherwise involving all institutional elements which would be included were the practice permanent. There is no institutional commitment to continue the innovation. The stage extends from the initial commitment to try the innovation to a review or evaluation of first results. *Refinement* moves the proposal from initial trial to the point of decision to continue innovative development, but with the purpose of sharpening its focus or design. Possible refinements emerge as a result of feedback from ongoing reviews. This stage ends with the adoption of the innovation as a permanent fea-

ture of the college. The *institutionalization* stage involves full acceptance of the innovation, including its movement into the regular operations of the institution. A new state of equilibrium has then been reached, institutionalization being closure of the developmental cycle. Although the time span for progression along this continuum from incipient exploration through total institutionalization may differ considerably from one change situation to another, the continuity or development of an innovation at any stage is a function or result of the interplay of various interactive forces.

4. The momentum of support for the innovation derived from all positive forces must outweigh the negative forces at each stage of development if the innovation is to progress to total institutionalization rather than stagnating for an undue time at an earlier stage or being terminated.

5. Specific forces have different importance at different developmental stages. For example, a decision maker may have a vital role to play during the exploration stage, while an implementor may have much greater importance during the trial stage.

6. The strength of the goal hiatus force derived from a given stated institutional goal is directly related to the aspiration or priority position given the goal in comparison with others; this is to say that a goal hiatus of certain value attached to a high aspiration or priority goal generates greater energy for change than that same hiatus value would if attached to a goal of lesser aspiration or priority position.

Numerical values may be assigned to each of these forces at each stage of development in order that the change leadership may assess the most important positive and negative pressures and deal with them by increasing the positive and reducing the negative forces.

A matrix provides a perceptual framework for visualizing these postulates of the theory in their entirety. It can serve as a mechanism for converting the abstract language of the theory into concrete form. Table 2 presents such a matrix, with the three categories of interactive forces listed along the vertical or "Y" axis, and the five categories of developmental stage along the horizontal "X" axis.

To apply the interactive forces theory to any particular in-

*Table 2.*

MATRIX FOR ASSESSING THE IMPACT OF INTERACTIVE
FORCES ON AN INNOVATION DURING ITS DEVELOPMENT

| *Interactive Forces* | *Developmental Stages* | | | | |
|---|---|---|---|---|---|
| | Explora-tion | Formula-tion | Trial | Refine-ment | Institution-alization |
| *Personal* (official decision makers, implementors, consumers) | | | | | |
| *Extrapersonal* (tangible resources and facilities; intangible trends, policies, and traditions) | | | | | |
| *Goal Hiatus* (discrepancy between goal aspiration and goal achievement) | | | | | |

novation, the cells of the matrix are filled by estimates of the strength and valence of each major force at each stage of development. That is, for each square or cell a value is computed reflecting the amount of positive or negative force likely to be exerted on the innovation at each stage, as estimated by those knowledgeable about the institution. For example, such groups of knowledgeable persons can identify the major personal and extrapersonal forces that will bear on the innovation in any particular stage. Each computed value in turn will have been derived from the pooled judgments of respondents representing the various constituencies of the college. A rating of −10, for example, might refer to the most powerful negative degree of influence; a rating of +10 could indicate the most powerful positive influence. Any force believed to render no influence on the change should simply be eliminated from the scoring procedure, for it is not in fact one of the interactive forces. For mathematical reasons explained in the Appendix a zero rating is not used. Next, all institutional goals to which the innovation has a demonstrable relationship can be identified and two ratings assigned to them: (1) a rating (from 1 to 10) of the institution's *aspiration* for the goal; (2) a rating (also from 1 to 10) depicting the level of institutional achievement of this goal. The numerical value separating these two ratings will indicate the hiatus between goal aspiration and goal achievement. Thus, a maximum aspiration rating of 10 for some particular goal that could be achieved by the innovation contrasted with a minimum achievement rating of 1 would be a hiatus of the strongest possible force for the proposed change. A neutral situation in terms of goal hiatus force would occur whenever the level of goal achievement equals the level of aspiration—for example, when both aspiration and achievement are rated identically and no discrepancy exists between them. Situations can exist where the level of aspiration for a particular goal is actually lower than its level of achievement—in which case no positive pressure exists for the innovation from this source, and instead negative pressure against it may be predicted.

At each developmental stage, the ratings for each of these forces (either positive or negative) can be aggregated to produce a resultant which gives an assessment of the total direction and extent of forces impinging on the plan. Thus, if the computed resultant of the several forces at any given stage is relatively low, either on the scale of absolute possible values or in relation to the resultants computed for the forces in the earlier stages, it is unlikely that the innovation will progress further without the intervention of the change agent or manager or some other factor to augment positive influences or to counteract forces blocking progress. (Explanation of the scoring procedure is presented in the Appendix.) Forces with low or negative values will alert the innovator to acquire compensatory support from other sources if the innovation is to proceed. Illustrations of such adjustments in leadership role are given in the hypothetical case presented later in this chapter.

While the matrix can be employed retrospectively to reconstruct the causes for the progress or failure of a past change, it can be even more valuable as a planning device for estimating the likely level of forces in the future regarding a projected innovation and for either taking preventing action with respect to the most critical forces or adapting the innovation to assure positive support for it. As a planning aid, the interactive forces theory and matrix parallels "management by exception" in the field of business management. There, as long as data provided by the management information system fall within predetermined limits, the operation proceeds "automatically." When the data fall short or exceed these limits, however, managers of the appropriate departments use this feedback information to deal with the "exception." Here, with the interactive forces theory, whenever the resultant of forces projected at a given developmental stage of an innovation fall toward zero or below, decision makers can take similar compensatory action to modify the total complex of forces in the positive direction or consider alternative innovations with greater likelihood of success.

## Deltec College: A Case Illustration

To assist change agents and change managers in using the ideas developed thus far, a composite case compiled from several actual institutions can illustrate the simulation and scoring techniques involved in the interactive forces theory. The case can illustrate also the way various tactics are used to implement a broad strategy which guides the institution as it seeks constructive change.

"Deltec College" is one of four state-supported and state-controlled two-year technical colleges operated by the state university of a western state. It has a history of excellent programs, particularly in occupational fields, and general agreement exists within the state university and the state board of education that Deltec and its sister colleges should move toward developing comprehensive programs leading to associate degrees in general education and in liberal arts and science transfer programs as well as occupational programs of technical and semiprofessional nature. Meanwhile, however, local comprehensive community colleges have been growing in number and enrollment throughout the state under a strong statewide plan; and many communities—including Beltsville, seven miles to the west and the closest city to Deltec—have expressed interest in creating their own community-controlled two-year institutions. The threat posed by the possible establishment of a community college nearby called for change leaders at Deltec to formulate a general strategy to counter such a possibility and to examine various tactics that might be followed to implement this strategy. The general strategy chosen was to make Deltec a comprehensive two-year college (as opposed to a technical institute) as soon as possible. Any action to move the institution toward comprehensiveness, then, would be viewed as a possibly useful tactic; but the need remained to determine which of several such tactics and related subtactics should be used.

In contrast to the community colleges, which aimed at meeting local community needs, policy makers at Deltec wanted it to become a comprehensive college at the associate-degree level, providing programs serving regional and statewide needs. This extension of the idea of comprehensiveness from a local to a broad and rich regional service was a part of Deltec's general strategy of "going the community college idea one better" and thereby gaining public favor in the total region. Changes in Deltec's operation seemed necessary to accomplish this aim, and in most instances not one but several alternative paths could be identified. By analyzing the potential forces (positive and negative) for each of these alternatives, Deltec's planners and policy makers could better predict the chances for successful implementation of each suggested change.

Three institutional goals of Deltec could be achieved by the alternative innovations described below. Two of these goals were well known not only in the region served by Deltec but also throughout the state: first, that it should become comprehensive in its programs, as noted above; second, that it should increase its regional identity by assuring service to its five surrounding counties —an area approximately one fourth of the total state. The third goal, carefully never stated in discussions involving persons outside Deltec or in documents publicizing its plans, was to develop programs which would undercut the need for local community colleges in Deltec's region. Already within Beltsville, a petition was being circulated for establishment of its own community college.

Two alternatives seemed viable in achieving these three goals: one, interinstitutional cooperation with two area vocational schools; the other, creation of a Beltsville vocational center. The most important interactive forces impinging on these two choices are described below. The Deltec president requested the executive vice-president to make a systematic examination of the two alternatives and to recommend a course of action. Now in the role of change manager, the executive vice-president decided to utilize the interactive forces theory and its matrix for analysis in order to draw broadly on the insights of knowledgeable people in the college and community.

*Alternative A: Interinstitutional cooperation with two area vocational schools.* Deltec could enter into agreements with two nearby area vocational schools, Northeast and Southern, that were operated by local boards of education in districts not traditionally served by Deltec but within its five-county region: one to the northeast about fifteen miles; the other to the south about twenty miles. Both of these schools served a network of surrounding cooperating public school districts and were heavily subsidized by the state for vocational education at the high school level. Both were legally empowered to offer adult and postsecondary vocational education but were restricted from awarding associate degrees. As yet, neither had acquired permanent physical facilities in which to operate their programs. If a consortium arrangement were effected with Deltec, their students would be able to earn a Deltec degree for appropriate work at Northeast or Southern.

The directors of the two schools differed about the idea of a consortium involving Deltec: Southern's favored the idea; Northeast's opposed it, preferring instead to expand Northeast's own facilities and programs through changes in state support and legislation. The state director of vocational education was enthusiastic about the idea; but his superior, the state commissioner of education, was worried about the adequacy of an interinstitutional approach. Both the state university president and the university's vice-president for technical colleges, who was administratively responsible for Deltec and its sister colleges, were opposed; they did not want to assume responsibility outside the collegiate level for programming over which they had little control.

In addition, three local chambers of commerce constituted important personal forces. Deltec's own chamber of commerce was neutral; Southern's chamber of commerce favored the consortium; and Northeast's chamber of commerce opposed it, believing that the community should grow on its own merits rather than as a satellite of the Deltec area. The same split separated the boards of control of the two vocational schools, with Southern's supportive and Northeast's wanting to expand Northeast into a comprehensive community college of the type feared by Deltec.

Table 3 identifies the three Deltec goals related to this plan; the individuals and groups likely to be influential in its implementation; and the extrapersonal forces impinging on it. The numbers in each cell are the pooled or average judgments of knowledgeable respondents who evaluated and reported to the change manager (in this case the Deltec executive vice-president) the estimated influence of each designated force at specified stages of development. From this matrix, it became obvious that much effort would need to be expended in gaining adequate support to institutionalize the consortium, particularly when compared with a second alternative.

*Alternative B: Establishing Beltsville Vocational Center.* In the opinion of many Deltec personnel, a former textile mill of substantial brick construction and large floor space located on a ten-acre site six miles from Deltec on the edge of Beltsville toward the campus should be used for a vocational center. The local advisory council had hoped to start such a center, and the faculty and counselors—reflecting student opinion—favored its creation. The vice-president for technical colleges in the state university saw it as a possible demonstration project of comprehensive programming for the four technical colleges. The executive director of the state board for community colleges was favorable because he wanted the community colleges to concentrate on local rather than regional services; and the Beltsville chamber of commerce was on record in favor of the center. However, a strong negative personal force was exerted initially by the state director for vocational education, who saw the possible center as a direct challenge to the area vocational schools and who was willing to work at local, regional, and state levels to prevent Deltec's acquisition of the textile mill.

Table 4 illustrates the judgment of other knowledgeable persons about the importance of each of these forces in effecting this alternative. In comparison with Table 3, fewer obstacles would need to be overcome to initiate this idea than that of cooperation with Northeast and Southern; in addition, if the center were to

Table 3.

MATRIX OF FORCES INVOLVED IN INTERINSTITUTIONAL
COOPERATION WITH TWO AREA VOCATIONAL SCHOOLS*

| Interactive forces | Developmental Stages | |
| --- | --- | --- |
| | Exploration | Formulation |
| **Personal** | | |
| Decision Makers | | |
| Deltec president | 5.1 | 5.4 |
| Deltec College council | 7.1 | 7.7 |
| State university vice-president for technical programs | −3.6 | −3.6 |
| State university president | −2.8 | −2.9 |
| State director of vocational education | 8.2 | 7.6 |
| State commissioner of education | 3.1 | 2.9 |
| Director, Southern Vocational School | 6.2 | 7.1 |
| Board of control, Southern Vocational | 6.3 | 6.9 |
| Director, Northeast Vocational School | −3.4 | −5.2 |
| Board of control, Northeast Vocational | −4.0 | −5.4 |
| Executive director, state board of community colleges | 5.4 | 5.5 |
| Implementors | | |
| Deltec faculty | 5.4 | 5.7 |
| Deltec counselors | 6.8 | 6.9 |
| Consumers | | |
| Deltec chamber of commerce | 3.7 | 3.7 |
| Southern chamber of commerce | 7.5 | 8.1 |
| Northeast chamber of commerce | −5.1 | −5.9 |
| **Extrapersonal** | | |
| Temporary facilities at Northeast and Southern | 3.9 | 3.9 |
| Federal grant for vocational program | — | 7.6 |
| Deltec policy to grant credit for vocational courses | 7.9 | 7.9 |
| Beltsville petition for community college | — | 8.0 |

## Table 3. (cont.)

### MATRIX OF FORCES INVOLVED IN INTERINSTITUTIONAL
### COOPERATION WITH TWO AREA VOCATIONAL SCHOOLS

| | Developmental Stages | | | |
| --- | --- | --- | --- | --- |
| Interactive forces | Exploration | | Formulation | |
| *Goal Hiatus* | | | | |
| Aspiration and achievement levels | Asp. | Ach. | Asp. | Ach. |
| To be comprehensive in programs—that is, to offer vocational, general, and liberal arts programs | 7.9 | 2.3 | 8.0 | 2.3 |
| To establish a regional identity within the five-county service region | 7.7 | 5.9 | 7.7 | 6.2 |
| To develop programs which will offset local pressure for creation of competing community colleges | 7.5 | 2.8 | 7.9 | 3.1 |
| Resultant Force Index | 1.22 | | 1.32 | |

NOTE: The figures in the columns represent the pooled judgments of respondents reporting to the change manager and representing the various constituencies of the college.

prove successful, Deltec's goals would be achieved more effectively. As a consequence, Deltec's policy makers recommended to the state university this alternative for implementation. The university president recommended, and the board of trustees approved, launching of the Beltsville experiment.

During the succeeding three years, the Beltsville center moved from the formulation stage through trial and into refinement, supported in part by special federal funds channeled through the state education department. Over this period, however, the idea of the Beltsville center was not fully institutionalized. The textile plant which housed it was merely leased by the university, which refused to provide a capital budget that would have made the center permanent; and the net effect of this refusal to buy the property was to postpone indefinitely any progress toward institutionalization. Now at the stage of refinement but with no obvious movement toward institutionalization, the change leadership at Deltec was faced with the need to examine anew alternative courses of action to maintain the momentum of the innovation.

This fact illustrates a second use of the interactive forces theory. A given innovation, such as the Beltsville center, may have little opportunity to become institutionalized if existing forces are allowed to run their course without active intervention by the innovator. Efforts to strengthen positive forces or to diminish negative forces must be undertaken if the innovation is to progress to maturation. By the end of the third year of the Beltsville center, Deltec's administrators had concluded that without some change in the pattern of interactive forces, the center would be likely to fail in its purposes. Some Beltsville citizens were expressing renewed interest in creating a local comprehensive community college, and another potential buyer for the textile mill had appeared.

Deltec's leaders decided, therefore, to try two new tactics to complete the Beltsville innovation and to maintain momentum in the anti-community college strategy: (1) involving as a positive force the state commissioner of education; (2) convincing the owner of the mill of the advantages to be gained from deeding the mill to Deltec. The commissioner of education, because of his elected position, was sensitive to political reality, including the expressed preferences of local constituents. Deltec's president and council arranged for the commissioner to visit and confer with the college administration and faculty regarding the Beltsville center and then to speak to local business, educational, and political groups about the value of such an innovation. This tactic did two things: it outflanked local opposition to the concept of a vocational center in Beltsville, and it reinforced the growing positive support for the center by the state director of vocational education, who reported to the commissioner of education. The second tactic aimed directly at removing the major roadblock to the maturation of the innovation—namely, the fact that the future of the textile mill was uncertain. Rather than continuing to try to persuade the university to include a capital item in its budget for the mill, Deltec's president and council decided to convince the mill owner that he should give the mill to Deltec at the end of a five-year period of demonstrated socially productive use of the facility. For the owner, such a gift

## Table 4.

## MATRIX OF FORCES INVOLVED IN ESTABLISHING BELTSVILLE VOCATIONAL CENTER

| Interactive Forces | Developmental Stages | | | |
| --- | --- | --- | --- | --- |
| | Exploration | Formulation | Trial | Refinement |
| *Personal* | | | | |
| Decision Makers | | | | |
| Deltec president | 8.6 | 8.7 | 9.1 | 9.1 |
| Deltec College council | 7.8 | 8.0 | 8.2 | 8.8 |
| State university vice-president for technical programs | 6.1 | 6.5 | 6.5 | 7.4 |
| State university president | 4.1 | 6.2 | 5.1 | 4.9 |
| State director of vocational education | −8.3 | −4.1 | 0.1 | 4.2 |
| Executive director, state board of community colleges | 6.3 | 6.7 | 7.0 | 7.8 |
| Implementors | | | | |
| Deltec faculty | 6.4 | 6.9 | 7.1 | 8.1 |
| Deltec counselors | 7.1 | 7.8 | 8.1 | 9.1 |

| | | Asp. | Ach. | Asp. | Ach. | Asp. | Ach. | Asp. | Ach. |
|---|---|---|---|---|---|---|---|---|---|
| **Consumers** | | | | | | | | | |
| Beltsville chamber of commerce | | 6.4 | | 6.8 | | 6.9 | | 7.6 | |
| *Extrapersonal* | | | | | | | | | |
| Availability of large building suitable for vocational programs | | 7.1 | | 7.3 | | 8.1 | | 8.9 | |
| Federal grant for the vocational program | | — | | — | | — | | 7.6 | |
| University opposition to capital investment | | — | | — | | — | | −2.0 | |
| Beltsville petition for community college | | — | | — | | — | | 8.0 | |
| *Goal Hiatus* | | | | | | | | | |
| Aspiration and achievement level | | Asp. | Ach. | Asp. | Ach. | Asp. | Ach. | Asp. | Ach. |
| To be comprehensive in programs—that is, to offer vocational, general, and liberal arts programs | | 7.9 | 2.3 | 8.0 | 3.3 | 8.1 | 3.9 | 9.0 | 6.6 |
| To establish a regional identity within the five-county service region | | 7.7 | 5.9 | 7.7 | 6.2 | 8.0 | 6.4 | 8.7 | 6.6 |
| To develop programs which will offset local pressure for creation of competing community colleges | | 7.5 | 2.8 | 7.9 | 5.1 | 7.9 | 5.3 | 8.6 | 6.5 |
| Resultant Force Index | | 1.54 | | 1.59 | | 1.71 | | 1.51 | |

NOTE: The figures in the columns represent the pooled judgments of respondents reporting to the change manager and representing the various constituencies of the college.

would be tax deductible; and for Deltec, the gift would secure the institutionalization of its Beltsville center. Knowing that the mill owner was the only direct heir of an old-line area family, with strong loyalties to the region, the president was able to prepare a persuasive case for the bequest.

Both of these tactics proved productive, as illustrated in Table 5. The state commissioner of education became a positive supporter of the center and defused local pressure for a competing community college; and the textile mill was promised to Deltec after two more years of successful operation. With these two changes, the Beltsville center now had the potential of proceeding to institutionalization and thus contributing substantially to Deltec's goals.

## Summary

Applying the interactive forces theory to a specific innovation, such as that illustrated by the Beltsville Vocational Center, should enable college and university decision makers to identify the most significant forces impinging on the innovation and forecast the effect of these forces on the likely development of the innovation. If the totality of forces does not show sufficiently high positive support for the innovation at any given stage of development, other positive forces must be brought to bear or existing ones strengthened and negative forces decreased if the innovation is to succeed. If these forces cannot be modified, some alternative innovation may be required. Similarly, if the positive forces wane over a period of time, compensatory action will be needed if the innovation is to remain viable.

Change agents and managers should be prepared for the likelihood that positive forces will indeed most likely wane as an innovation develops. At an early point in this study, we assumed that the total numerical score representing the collective interacting forces would tend to increase in a positive direction as the development moved toward maturity. But field observation thus far tends to lead to another hypothesis, perhaps because an innovation, as it develops, moves the institution closer and closer to achieving its goals and thus reduces the hiatus between aspiration and achievement; in such a case positive forces often seem to surge and peak during the first three stages of exploration, formulation, and trial, then level or decline during refinement and institutionalization. As was illustrated by the Deltec case in this chapter, a redoubling of effort may be necessary in the latter stages of development if this phenomenon of "surge/peak/fall" is not to halt the maturation of the change.

Colleges and universities, if they are to fulfill their obligations, cannot remain static during rapidly changing times. They must adapt as social pressures shift. But if they are to do more than merely respond to external pressures, if they are instead to shape these pressures, they will require a more theoretical understanding of the forces of academic change. Lester Anderson phrases the problem well: "The fundamental purpose of colleges and universities . . . is to be a knowledge and culture carrier or conserver or transmitter; a knowledge producer, discoverer, or creator. . . . Higher education needs and warrants careful study, as in this century it has become pervasive, exceedingly complex, and immensely costly. Society now *demands* that colleges and universities be responsible and accountable. But the responsibility and accounting can only be rendered and understood as the goals, the structures, and the governance mechanisms of colleges and universities are also understood" (1973, p. 2).

Higher education must pursue its proven functions of advancing the general society through the application of scholarship and knowledge to the resolution of human problems, through constantly challenging established views in all fields in order to generate better knowledge, and through preparing the reservoir of able individuals with specialized knowledge for leadership in all fields that the future demands.

Scholars and decision makers at other major social institutions are increasingly using theoretical concepts and frameworks to understand their own institutions. By and large, however, decision makers within higher education have relied on descriptive and empirical techniques to understand colleges and universities. As a result, their understanding and their ability to respond to change have been limited. For example, many of them continue to see forces bearing on their institutions as single pressures isolated one from the other, rather than as an interacting network of forces of which institutional change is a function.

## Table 5.

### MATRIX OF FORCES INVOLVED IN INSTITUTIONALIZING THE BELTSVILLE VOCATIONAL CENTER

| Interactive Forces | Developmental Stages | | | | |
|---|---|---|---|---|---|
| | Exploration | Formulation | Trial | Refinement | Institu- tionalization |
| *Personal* | | | | | |
| Decision Makers | | | | | |
| Deltec president | 8.6 | 8.7 | 9.1 | 9.1 | 9.2 |
| Deltec College council | 7.8 | 8.0 | 8.2 | 8.8 | 8.7 |
| State university vice-president for technical programs | 6.1 | 6.5 | 6.5 | 7.4 | 8.3 |
| State university president | 4.1 | 6.2 | 5.1 | 6.4 | 7.9 |
| State director of vocational education | −8.3 | 1.0 | 5.6 | 7.2 | 7.5 |
| Executive director, state board of community colleges | 6.3 | 6.7 | 7.0 | 7.8 | 7.9 |
| State Commissioner of Education | — | 6.3 | 6.7 | 7.5 | 8.1 |
| Implementors | | | | | |
| Deltec faculty | 6.4 | 6.9 | 7.1 | 8.1 | 8.0 |
| Deltec counselors | 7.1 | 7.8 | 8.1 | 9.1 | 9.2 |
| Consumers | | | | | |
| Beltsville Chamber of Commerce | 6.4 | 6.8 | 6.9 | 7.6 | 7.9 |

*Extrapersonal*

| | Asp. | Ach. | Asp. | Ach. | Asp. | Ach. | Asp. | Ach. | Asp. | Ach. |
|---|---|---|---|---|---|---|---|---|---|---|
| Availability of large building suitable for vocational program | 7.1 | | 7.3 | | 8.1 | | | | 8.9 | 8.9 |
| Federal grant for vocational program | | | | | | | | | 7.7 | 7.6 |
| University opposition to capital investment | | | | | | | | | — | −2.0 |
| Beltsville petition for community college | | | | | | | | | 7.6 | 8.0 |
| Commitment from owner to deed textile mill to Deltec in two years | | | | | | | | | 8.9 | 7.5 |

*Goal Hiatus*

| Aspiration and achievement levels | Asp. | Ach. | Asp. | Ach. | Asp. | Ach. | Asp. | Ach. | Asp. | Ach. |
|---|---|---|---|---|---|---|---|---|---|---|
| To be comprehensive in programs—that is, to offer vocational, general, and liberal arts programs | 7.9 | 2.3 | 8.0 | 3.3 | 8.1 | 3.9 | 9.0 | 6.6 | 9.0 | 8.1 |
| To establish a regional identity within the five-county service area | 7.7 | 5.9 | 7.7 | 6.2 | 8.0 | 6.4 | 8.7 | 6.6 | 8.9 | 7.7 |
| To develop programs which will offset local pressure for creation of competing community colleges | 7.5 | 2.8 | 7.9 | 5.1 | 7.9 | 5.3 | 8.6 | 6.5 | 9.1 | 7.5 |
| Resultant Force Index | 1.54 | | 1.65 | | 1.76 | | 1.60 | | 1.78 | |

NOTE: The figures in the columns represent the pooled judgments of respondents reporting to the change manager and representing the various constituencies of the college.

Questions about the possible effects of change deserve answers. How do state-level agencies designed to coordinate higher education affect the stimulation or the suppression of innovation? How can faculty responsibility and freedom for the viability of programming and instruction best be maintained? Can some colleges have as their basic purpose innovation and experimentation as such, in hopes of generating changes in neighboring institutions, or do such unusual institutions have the opposite effect of isolating themselves from potential emulation? Theories about institutional change, such as the interactive forces theory presented here, aim to form a basis for successful change in higher education. They cannot substitute for the enthusiasm and dedication illustrated by the innovators of new programs and institutions in Chapters Two through Five. But they can permit better answers to questions about the future of higher education, and they can offer innovators an analytic tool for making their enthusiasm and dedication more effective and their ideas more successful.

# Appendix

# Possible Scoring Procedure for Analyzing Interactive Forces

$P$ersons or groups of persons knowledgeable about the overall setting of an institution, its traditions and operations, and an innovation under consideration provide the input to the matrix for the interactive forces theory. They are asked to carry out five procedures, using their knowledge of the situation and the matrix worksheet (see Chapter Eight): (1) to identify any stages of development through which the innovation has already progressed; (2) to identify all personal and extrapersonal forces which bear on the status of the innovation in the institution during each stage; (3) to identify all institutional goals to which the innovation has a demonstrable relationship during any one or more of its stages; (4) to assign each goal at each stage a rating of 1 to 10 to depict

**197**

the strength of the institutional aspiration toward that goal, with a rating of 10 for a goal of utmost primacy, and to assign each goal a similar rating of 1 to 10 to depict the level to which the goal has been achieved, with a rating of 10 for a goal considered to be fully and satisfactorily achieved; and (5) to assign to each identified personal and extrapersonal force a rating from −10 to +10 to show its degree of influence, with a rating of +10 being most positively powerful and −10 most negatively powerful. In the scoring procedure described here, zero is not used because it would depict no influence and as such would be gratuitous among the interactive forces (it would represent no force at all).

After the ratings are assigned they must be combined. For purposes of illustration, three personal forces $(A, B, C)$, three extrapersonal forces $(a, b, c)$, and three institutional goal hiatus forces $(X, Y, \zeta)$ are used. The mathematical task at hand is then to combine ratings of each of these so that for each developmental stage (for which ratings are assigned by several raters) a single index figure can be calculated to show the raters' collective judgment of the resultant of all interactive forces. For purposes of illustration, let us assume that five raters are involved. The mathematical steps and the explanation for each follow.

Let us assume that the ratings assigned for a given stage are those in Table 1. The calculation of the resultant is indicated

*Table 1.*

INTERACTIVE FORCES

| Rater | Personal Forces | | | Extrapersonal Forces | | | Goal Hiatus Forces Aspiration and Achievement Levels | | | | | |
|---|---|---|---|---|---|---|---|---|---|---|---|---|
| | | | | | | | X | | Y | | Z | |
| | A | B | C | a | b | c | Asp. | Ach. | Asp. | Ach. | Asp. | Ach. |
| 1 | 10 | 9 | 3 | 6 | 4 | 10 | 10 | 8 | 6 | 2 | 5 | 3 |
| 2 | 9 | 6 | 5 | 9 | 2 | 8 | 10 | 7 | 7 | 4 | 7 | 4 |
| 3 | 8 | 6 | 4 | 7 | 3 | 10 | 9 | 6 | 6 | 4 | 5 | 4 |
| 4 | 9 | 7 | 3 | 6 | 5 | 9 | 10 | 8 | 7 | 2 | 6 | 4 |
| 5 | 10 | 8 | 2 | 8 | 3 | 9 | 9 | 7 | 8 | 5 | 6 | 3 |

below. In these equations the numerator for each fraction contains the assigned rating, and the denominator contains the maximum possible positive force, +10. Note that the denominators of these fractions must be summations $(\Sigma)$, just as the numerators are, so that we can compare the total assigned ratings to the total possible positive ratings. The same result may be achieved by taking the average of the assigned ratings over, or in relation to, the total of the maximum positive ratings.

Personal forces are derived as follows:

$$A = \frac{\Sigma\ 10 +\ 9 +\ 8 +\ 9 + 10}{\Sigma\ 10 + 10 + 10 + 10 + 10} = \frac{46}{50}$$

$$B = \frac{\Sigma\ 9 +\ 6 +\ 6 +\ 7 +\ 8}{\Sigma\ 10 + 10 + 10 + 10 + 10} = \frac{36}{50}$$

$$C = \frac{\Sigma\ 3 +\ 5 +\ 4 +\ 3 +\ 2}{\Sigma\ 10 + 10 + 10 + 10 + 10} = \frac{17}{50}$$

$$A + B + C = \frac{\Sigma\ 46 + 36 + 17}{\Sigma\ 50 + 50 + 50} = \frac{99}{150} = 0.66$$

Using the same procedure, the following values for extrapersonal forces can be derived:

$a = 36/50;\ b = 17/50;\ c = 46/50;\ a + b + c = 99/150 = 0.66.$

In our scoring approach, the maximum possible positive score, +10, is the same for both personal and extrapersonal forces. Because of this constant in the formula, in practice simpler procedures than those given above, such as taking the mean $(\overline{X})$, may be used to determine the influence of, for example, personal forces. To illustrate:

$$
\begin{aligned}
A &= 10 + 9 + 8 + 9 + 10 = 46 & \overline{X} &=\ 9.2 \\
B &=\ 9 + 6 + 6 + 7 +\ 8 = 36 & \overline{X} &=\ 7.2 \\
C &=\ 3 + 5 + 4 + 3 +\ 2 = 17 & \overline{X} &=\ 3.4 \\
& \qquad\qquad\qquad\ \Sigma = 99 & & 19.8
\end{aligned}
$$

$\overline{X} = 99/150 = 0.66$ or $19.8/30 = 0.66$

$A + B + C = 0.66$

This illustration shows the ratings assigned by five respondents, averaged to obtain a mean value for the whole group's rating of the influence of three forces on an innovation at a particular developmental stage. If more than one group is included in a rating exercise, a mean may be obtained for each group and a mean of means calculated to represent for that developmental stage the influence of interactive forces as rated by all respondents.

For illustration, we assume that equal weight is given to the ratings of all respondents and likewise to all three categories and subcategories of interactive forces. Unequal weighting of forces or respondents would be appropriate for testing a research hypothesis in which, for example, extrapersonal forces were believed to be stronger than personal forces.

The range of influence of personal or extrapersonal forces consists of the open interval $-1.00$ to $+1.00$ since in the formula utilized the most negative force is depicted as

$$\frac{-10}{+10} = -1.00,$$

and the most positive force as

$$\frac{+10}{+10} = +1.00.$$

Deriving the central tendency for a group of forces, or for the ratings of those forces by a group of respondents, does not alter the range of potential values for either personal or extrapersonal interactive forces.

Determining the hiatus, or difference between aspiration and achievement, in goal orientation is complicated, for it must be related to all the varying levels of aspiration possible. A hiatus that is equal to another is a greater force for change if the goal it describes is more highly aspired to. The general formula for depicting this relation is

$$\text{goal hiatus force} = \frac{T(T\text{–}D)}{\max T(\max T - \min D)}$$

where $T$ = assigned aspiration rating
$D$ = assigned achievement rating
$\max T$ = maximum possible aspiration rating (always 10)
$\min D$ = minimum possible achievement rating (always 1)

Using this formula, we first determine the force for change of a goal hiatus of a particular value by relating it to the level of aspiration toward that goal. For example, two sets of aspiration and achievement ratings, 10 and 8 and 5 and 3, show a hiatus value of $2(10 - 8$ and $5 - 3)$. But to determine its force for change, the hiatus must be related to the aspiration level by multiplication, as shown in the numerator of the formula. Then, to arrive at the total goal hiatus force, we derive the ratio of this product to the maximum possible hiatus force, which is shown in the denominator. This maximum value is a constant: $10(10 - 1) = 90$.

The goal hiatus force for goal $X$ may be determined as follows:

$$\frac{\Sigma}{\Sigma} \frac{10(10-8)+10(10-7)+9(9-6)+10(10-8)+9(9-7)}{90 \ + \ 90 \ + 90 \ + \ 90 \ + 90} =$$

$$\frac{20 + 30 + 27 + 20 + 18}{90 + 90 + 90 + 90 + 90} = \frac{115}{450} = 0.26$$

Using the same procedure, we derive the following values for goal $Y$:

$116/450 = 0.26$; and for goal $Z$: $66/450 = 0.15$. The total:

$$X + Y + Z = \frac{115 + 116 + \ 66}{450 + 450 + 450} = \frac{297}{1350} = 0.22$$

Again note that all denominators and all numerators must be summations. In practice, the calculations given above can be simplified in the same manner we indicated earlier for personal and extrapersonal forces.

The range of possible values for the goal hiatus force is from 0.00 to +1.00 as long as the level of aspiration for the goal is higher than the level of achievement. This range is shown by using the formula with values for maximum aspiration and maximum achievement (that is, 10 and 10) and with values for maximum aspiration and minimum achievement (10 and 1).

In the latter the force for change is the greatest possible for any combination of aspiration and achievement. The two extremes of the range of values are illustrated by the following two equations:

$$\frac{10(10-10)}{90} = \frac{0}{90} = 0.00$$

$$\frac{10(10-1)}{90} = \frac{90}{90} = +1.00$$

A neutral force level (zero) occurs whenever the level of achievement equals the level of aspiration, not just when achievement equals 10 and aspiration equals 10. With aspiration and achievement levels of 3, for example,

$$\frac{3(3-3)}{90} = \frac{0}{90} = 0.00$$

The range of values for the goal hiatus force when the level of aspiration for the goal is lower than the level of achievement is from 0.00 to −0.28. The latter figure represents the most negative possible goal hiatus force, which occurs when the level of aspiration is 5 and the level of achievement is 10:

$$\frac{5(5-10)}{90} = \frac{-25}{90} = -0.28$$

In comparison, when the level of aspiration is only 1, even though the level of achievement is 10, the result is a smaller negative goal hiatus force, −0.10:

$$\frac{1(1-10)}{90} = \frac{-9}{90} = -0.10$$

As with personal and extrapersonal forces, obtaining the central tendency for a set of goal hiatus forces or for the judgments of a group of respondents does not alter the range of possible values.

The index of all forces (the resultant force index) impinging on the hypothetical innovation at the particular developmental stage illustrated here is derived as follows:

personal + extrapersonal + goal hiatus = resultant force index

0.66    +    0.66    +    0.22    =    1.54

In this fashion, the aggregate influence of the three forces can be assayed as they function together in each stage. The resultant index permits the testing of such hypotheses as that personal factors are more critical than extrapersonal ones or that they are more critical in certain stages but not in others.

As indicated above, the range of possible values for both personal and extrapersonal forces is from $-1.00$ to $+1.00$. For the goal hiatus forces the range is from $-0.28$ to $+1.00$. The range of possible values for the resultant force index, derived by adding positive and negative limits, is therefore from $-2.28$ to $+3.00$.

The resultant force index for any developmental stage of an innovation can be compared with that calculated for all other developmental stages to indicate the waxing or waning strength of all forces together. If calculated and applied by knowledgeable raters, the resultant force index can be used to predict the aggregate strength of all interactive forces and to test such predictions against experience.

# Bibliography

ANDERSON, G. L. "Does the Difference Make a Difference?" *Faculty Forum* (College of Education, Pennsylvania State University), April 1973, *12*, 1–4.

APPLEBAUM, R. *Theories of Social Change*. Chicago: Markham, 1970.

ASHBY, E. "The Structure of Higher Education: A World View." *AGB Reports*, 1973, *15*, 17–22.

ASHBY, E. *Adapting Universities to a Technological Society*. San Francisco: Jossey-Bass, 1974.

BAILEY, S. K. "Flexible Time-Space Programs: A Plea for Caution." In D. W. Vermilye (Ed.), *The Expanded Campus: Current Issues in Higher Education*. San Francisco: Jossey-Bass, 1972.

BASKIN, S. (Ed.) *Higher Education: Some Newer Developments*. New York: McGraw-Hill, 1965.

BECKHARD, R. *Organization Development: Strategies and Models*. Reading, Mass.: Addison-Wesley, 1969.

BELL, D. *The Coming of Post-Industrial Society*. New York: Basic Books, 1973.

**205**

BENNIS, W., BENNE, K., AND CHIN, R. (Eds.) *The Planning of Change.* New York: Holt, 1961.

BERND, DANIEL. "Prolegomenon to a Definition of Interdisciplinary Studies: The Experience at Governors State University." *Bulletin* of the Association of Departments of English, Dec. 1971.

BLOCKER, D., BENDER, L., AND MARTORANA, S. V. "The Politics of Postsecondary Education." Unpublished manuscript. 1974.

BLOOM, B. "Learning for Mastery." *Evaluation Comment* (UCLA Center for Study of Evaluation of Instructional Programs), 1968, *1*, 1–12.

BLOOM, B., AND OTHERS. *A Taxonomy of Educational Objectives.* New York: David McKay, 1964.

BOGARD, L. "Management in Institutions of Higher Education." In A. Wood and others, *Papers on Efficiency in Higher Education.* Berkeley: Carnegie Commission on Higher Education, 1972.

BRICK, M., AND MC GRATH, E. J. *Innovation in Liberal Arts Colleges.* New York: Teachers College Press, 1969.

Cabinet Committee on Cable Communications. *Report to the President.* Washington, D.C.: Government Printing Office, 1974.

Carnegie Commission on Higher Education. *Less Time, More Options —Education Beyond High School.* New York: McGraw-Hill, 1971.

Carnegie Commission on Higher Education. *The Fourth Revolution: Instructional Technology in Higher Education.* New York: Carnegie Foundation, 1972a.

Carnegie Commission on Higher Education. *Reform on Campus.* New York: McGraw-Hill, 1972b.

CHEIT, E. *The New Depression in Higher Education.* New York: McGraw-Hill, 1972.

Commission on Non-traditional Study. *Diversity by Design.* San Francisco: Jossey-Bass, 1973.

Cornell University, Center for Improvement of Undergraduate Education. *A Guide to Innovation in Higher Education.* New Rochelle: *Change* Magazine, 1974.

CORSON, J. J. *Governance of Colleges and Universities.* New York: McGraw-Hill, 1960.

CROSS, K. P. *Beyond the Open Door: New Students to Higher Education.* San Francisco: Jossey-Bass, 1971.

CROSS, K. P. "Serving the New Clientele for Postsecondary Education." Speech given at annual meeting of North Central Association of Colleges and Secondary Schools. Chicago, March 27, 1973.

DAHRENDORF, R. "Toward a Theory of Social Conflict." In W. Bennis, K. Benne, and R. Chin (Eds.), *The Planning of Change.* New York: Holt, 1961. Pp. 445–451.

DRESSEL, P. L. (Ed.) *The New Colleges: Toward an Appraisal.* Iowa City: American College Testing Program and American Association for Higher Education, 1971.

DRUCKER, P. F. *The Age of Discontinuity: Guidelines to Our Changing Society.* New York: Harper, 1969.

FAURE, E., AND OTHERS. *Learning to Be: The World of Education Today and Tomorrow.* Paris and Toronto: UNESCO and Ontario Institute for Studies in Education, 1973.

GAFF, J. G., AND ASSOCIATES. *The Cluster College.* San Francisco: Jossey-Bass, 1970.

GINSBERG, E. *Strategies for Educational Reform.* Columbus: Ohio State University, Center for Vocational and Technical Education, 1973.

GOULD, S. B. "Less Talk, More Action." In D. Vermilye (Ed.), *The Expanded Campus.* San Francisco: Jossey-Bass, 1972.

HAMPTON, D. R., SUMMER, C., AND WEBBER, R. A. *Organizational Behavior and the Practice of Management.* Glenview, Ill.: Scott, Foresman, 1968.

HARRIS, L. "The Harris Survey." *Washington Post,* Aug. 23, 1973.

HATCH, W. R. *The CRUX, Involvement of Students in Their Learning.* Corvallis: Oregon State University Press, 1974.

HEFFERLIN, JB L. *Dynamics of Academic Reform.* San Francisco: Jossey-Bass, 1969.

HEFFERLIN, JB L. "Hauling Academic Trunks." In C. Walker (Ed.), *Elements Involved in Academic Change.* Washington, D.C.: Association of American Colleges, 1972.

HEILBRONER, R. *An Inquiry into the Human Prospect.* New York: Norton, 1974.

HEISS, A. *An Inventory of Academic Innovation and Reform.* Berkeley: Carnegie Commission on Higher Education, 1973.

HERTZLER, J. O. *Social Institutions.* Lincoln: University of Nebraska Press, 1947.

HIRSCHMAN, A. O. *Exit, Voice, and Loyalty: Responses to Decline in Firms, Organizations, and States.* Cambridge, Mass.: Harvard University Press, 1970.

HODGKINSON, H. *Institutions in Transition.* Berkeley: Carnegie Commission on Higher Education, 1971.

HODGKINSON, H., AND BLOY, M. *Identity Crisis in Higher Education.* San Francisco: Jossey-Bass, 1971.

HOLM, D. S. "The Management of Change in Higher Education." *Professional File,* June 1972, *3,* 2.

HOULE, C. O. *The External Degree.* San Francisco: Jossey-Bass, 1973.

HOULE, C. O. "Implications of a Learning Society." In E. Kuhns and O. Toro (Eds.), *The Public Library: Catalyst for Adult Learning.* New York: College Entrance Examination Board, n.d.

HOYT, K. B. "Career Education: Challenges for Innovation in Community Colleges." Speech given at 30th annual community college conference, Texas A & M University, College Station, Texas, Oct. 15, 1973.

IKENBERRY, S. O., AND FRIEDMAN, R. C. *Beyond Academic Departments.* San Francisco: Jossey-Bass, 1972.

*Innovation.* Leaflet published by the League for Innovation in the Community College, Los Angeles, California, 1972.

JENCKS, C., AND RIESMAN, D. *The Academic Revolution.* Garden City, N.Y.: Doubleday, 1969.

KOOS, L. V. *Integrating High School and College: The 6-4-4 Plan at Work.* New York: Harper, 1947.

KUHN, A. *The Logic of Social Systems.* San Francisco: Jossey-Bass, 1974.

KUHNS, E. "The Modular Calendar: Catalyst for Change." *Educational Record,* 1974, *55* (1), 57–62.

KUHNS, E., AND MARTORANA, S. V. "Of Time and Modules: The Organization of Instruction." *Journal of Higher Education,* 1974, *45* (6), 430–440.

LESLIE, L., MARTORANA, S. V., AND FIFE, J. "Financing Post-Secondary Education Through Students: Windfall Profit or Recession for Community Colleges?" *Community College Review,* Winter 1975.

LEVINE, A., AND WEINGART, J. *Reform of Undergraduate Education.* San Francisco: Jossey-Bass, 1973.

LEVINGER, G. "Kurt Lewin's Approach to Conflict and Its Resolution." In W. Bennis, K. Benne, and R. Chin (Eds.), *The Planning of Change.* New York: Holt, 1961.

LEWIN, K. *A Dynamic Theory of Personality.* New York: McGraw-Hill, 1935.

LEWIN, K. "Quasi-Stationary Social Equilibria and the Problem of Permanent Change." In W. Bennis, K. Benne, and R. Chin

(Eds.), *The Planning of Change*. New York: Holt, 1961. Pp. 235–238.

LIKERT, R. *New Pattern of Management*. New York: McGraw-Hill, 1961.

LIPPITT, G. "What Do We Know About Leadership?" In W. Bennis, K. Benne, and R. Chin (Eds.), *The Planning of Change*. New York: Holt, 1961. Pp. 431–435.

MAC DONALD, G. B. (Ed.) *Five Experimental Colleges*. New York: Harper, 1973.

MARTORANA, S. V. *State-Level Planning for Community Colleges*. Iowa City: American College Testing Program, 1974.

MARTORANA, S. V., KUHNS, E., WITTER, R., AND STURTZ, A. *CUPIR: Cooperative Utilization of Private Institutional Resources*. University Park: Center for the Study of Higher Education, Pennsylvania State University, 1975.

MAYHEW, L. "Jottings." *Change*, 1973a, *5* (3), 63–64.

MAYHEW, L. *The Carnegie Commission on Higher Education: A Critical Analysis of the Reports and Recommendations*. San Francisco: Jossey-Bass, 1973b.

MAYHEW, L., AND FORD, P. *Changing the Curriculum*. San Francisco: Jossey-Bass, 1971.

MILLER, R. "Planning and the 'Measurable Objective.'" *Planning for Higher Education*, 1973, *2*, 1–3.

MOOD, A. M. *The Future of Higher Education*. New York: McGraw-Hill, 1973.

MOOD, A. M., AND OTHERS. *Papers on Efficiency in the Management of Higher Education*. Berkeley: Carnegie Commission on Higher Education, 1972.

MOORE, M. G. "Toward a Theory of Independent Learning and Teaching." *Journal of Higher Education*, 1973, *44*, 661–679.

NEWMAN, F., AND OTHERS. *Report on Higher Education*. Washington, D.C.: U.S. Department of Health, Education, and Welfare, 1971.

PACE, R. *The Demise of Diversity?* Berkeley: Carnegie Commission on Higher Education, 1974.

PARSONS, T. *The Social System*. New York: Free Press, 1951.

PARSONS, T., AND PLATT, G. *The American University*. Cambridge, Mass.: Harvard University Press, 1973.

PATTERSON, F. *Colleges in Consort: Institutional Cooperation Through Consortia*. San Francisco: Jossey-Bass, 1974.

PATTERSON, L. D. *1973 Consortium Directory*. Washington, D.C.: American Association for Higher Education, 1973.

POMES, C. E. "La Investigacion Cientifica: Un Metodo Docente Esencial en la Ensencial de las Profesiones Universitarias." *Revista de la Asociacion Latinoamericana de Facultades de Odontologia*, 1968, *3* (2), 127–148.

*Programa Regional de Desarrollo Educativo*. Washington, D.C.: Organization of American States, 1971.

REINERT, P. C. "Reform or Perish." *AGB Reports*, Nov.–Dec. 1972, pp. 16–22.

RIESMAN, D. *Constraint and Variety in American Education*. Garden City, N.Y.: Doubleday, 1958.

RIESMAN, D., AND STADTMAN, V. A. (Eds.) *Academic Transformation: Seventeen Institutions Under Pressure*. New York: McGraw-Hill, 1973.

RIVLIN, A. *Systematic Thinking for Social Action*. Washington, D.C.: Brookings Institute, 1971.

RUSSELL, E. *Measurement of Change Orientation of Vocational Teachers*. Columbus: Center for Vocational and Technical Education, Ohio State University, 1972.

SAGAN, H. "Organizational Reform Is Not Enough." In C. Walker (Ed.), *Elements Involved in Academic Change*. Washington, D.C.: Association of American Colleges, 1972.

SCHON, D. A. *Technology and Change: The Impact of Invention and Innovation on American Social and Economic Development*. New York: Delacorte Press, 1967.

SCHON, D. A. *Beyond the Stable State*. New York: Random House, 1971.

SHORES, L. "Public Library U.S.A.: An Essay in Comparative Librarianship." In R. F. Vollans (Ed.), *Libraries for the People: International Studies in Librarianship*. London: Library Association, 1968.

SNOW, C. *Two Cultures: And a Second Look*. New York: Cambridge University Press, 1969.

STEARNS, H. L. *Community Relations and the Public Schools*. Englewood Cliffs, N.J.: Prentice-Hall, 1955.

SUCZEK, R. F. *The Best Laid Plans: A Study of Student Development in an Experimental College Program*. San Francisco: Jossey-Bass, 1972.

TAYLOR, H. *How to Change Colleges: Notes on Radical Reform*. New York: Holt, 1971.

VERMILYE, D. W. (Ed.) *The Expanded Campus.* San Francisco: Jossey-Bass, 1972.

WHITLOCK, B. "Simon's Rock." *Community and Junior College Journal,* 1974, *44,* 18–20.

WILSON, L. *Shaping American Higher Education.* Washington, D.C.: American Council on Education, 1972.

ZIMMER, R. "Opportunity for Learning." *Community and Junior College Journal,* 1970, *40* (7), 48–56.

# Index

**213**